DESIGNING THE BRAND IDENTITY IN RETAIL SPACES

FAIRCHILD BOOKS

Designing the Brand Identity in Retail Spaces

MARTIN M. PEGLER

FAIRCHILD BOOKS
An Imprint of Bloomsbury Publishing Inc
BLOOMSBURY
LONDON • NEW DELHI • NEW YORK • SYDNEY

Fairchild Books

An imprint of Bloomsbury Publishing Inc

1385 Broadway
New York
NY 10018
USA

50 Bedford Square
London
WC1B 3DP
UK

www.fairchildbooks.com

First published 2015

Library of Congress Cataloging-in-Publication Data
A catalog record for this book is available from the Library of Congress

Pegler, Martin M.
Designing the brand identity in retail spaces / Martin M. Pegler.
pages cm
1. Stores, Retail. 2. Industrial design coordination. 3. Branding (Marketing).
4. Trademarks–Design. I. Title.
NA6220.P44 2015
725'.21–dc23
2014029269

ISBN: PB: 978-1-62892-391-9

Typeset by Saxon Graphics Ltd, Derby

Cover Design by Untitled

Contents

Extended Contents

PART 4: A BRAND STATEMENT 219

Introduction

Corporations, both large and small, spend great time, effort, and money on creating, projecting, and protecting their brand and their image to the public. Worldwide, billions are spent on advertising the brand—putting that image before an audience with the hopes of attracting a targeted part of that market. Companies get graphic artists to design the look of the brand, select a signature color, a specific font, a quirky logo design—anything that will make the representation of their brand unique, appealing, and memorable to that specific audience.

When that corporation invites the public into its domain, be it a retail store, a trade show, a café or restaurant, a bank, a corporate headquarters—anywhere where the public meets the brand in its own territory—how is the corporate brand made evident in that specific environment? Is it by use of the signature color that highlights the space, or the logo that reminds you over and over again where you are or, is it done more subtly with textures, forms, and related graphic cues? Does the brand or the brand concept change with each new locale or does the design concept adapt the brand image to the new country or new part of the world? How does the brand present itself in a foreign land in a new language? How does it involve the shopper's emotion or senses? It takes close cooperation with brand management and a visual sensitivity to turn the brand that is stated in words and goals into dimensional surroundings. It is the trained architect, interior designer, or store designer who can get that message across.

Collected in this volume are examples of many branded environments from around the world. Some are familiar brand names; some are recognized only in their particular part of the globe. What they all have in common is that they are open to the public, and in obvious or in subtle ways have provided the desired ambience for the client that reinforce the brand, its logo, and what the brand stands for. They have appealed to the senses and the emotions of the targeted shopper. The quotes, from the architects and designers who have created these memorable spaces, provide the reader with the "how, what, and why" of each project.

Why *now* a book on branded retail environments? Because, although we are inundated with books on the importance of the brand and branding, little attention has been paid to how brand identity plays an important part in retailing today. To define the terms "brand" and "brand identity," let me quote from a new book on branding: *Designing B2B Brands: Lessons from Deloitte and 195,000 Brand Managers*, by Carlos Martinez Onaindia and Brian Resnick (Wiley, 2013). "A brand is a collection of distinguishing and intangible assets that are most commonly associated with and shaped by a product, person, or organization, but eventually defined by the consumer or the audience."

From there, Brian Resnick, the co-author, goes on to define brand identity:

> *Brand identity is expressed through the most physically embodied aspects of the organization. It is the manifestation of the brand that can be seen, heard and immediately experienced. As part of a strategically integrated system of design and communication, the brand identity has the ability to impress and imprint—to distinguish the organization and build an appetite for future interaction. Brand identity encompasses visual identity, aural identity, and other sensory components of a brand.*

It is like walking into a shop and seeing, feeling, and being totally involved in—and surrounded by—the brand imagery. Brand identity is about adding emotional and sensory appeal to the brand.

What I am attempting to do in this book, by using the words of the designers themselves, is to show the creative process involved and explain how the brand identity or image is created in public spaces. For some spaces, the architect or designer worked with the client in creating the brand from just a starting conversation, then turning the concept into a 3-D reality. For other projects shown, the creative designers and architects have updated or upmarketed existing brands in order to capture another market or appeal to a different clientele. Still other projects introduce well-known or barely known brands into new markets or new countries, which may call for a different approach or design vocabulary, while other projects identify brands known only in their parts of the globe. Some architects/designers have been called upon to create prototype designs for the brand that will be adapted to suit a variety of spaces and locations and yet bring the essence of the brand with it. The "look" means continuity and goodwill; and the brand's reputation is represented by colors, materials, and visual cues that are inherent in the design wherever an outpost will be located. What all the projects have in common is that they are open to the public and in obvious or subtle ways have provided the desired ambience that reinforces the brand, the logo, and what the brand stands for.

For the spaces in this collection I have selected everything from designer or top fashion boutiques, to popular department stores, both large and small stores, showrooms, shops-within-shops and pop-up shops, trade show stands, exhibits, cafés and restaurants—the gamut of retail experiences and in a variety of markets and countries.

The book has been divided into four parts and each one refers to a different aspect of branding. We start with "A Brand Is Born" in which a new brand is introduced into the market. "A Brand Makeover" follows, in which established brands make changes in their brand concept and identity for various reasons. "A Brand Travels" shows how the brand adapts to new cities, countries, or cultures. The final part is devoted to "A Brand Statement," where established brands proudly present themselves to the public.

So, enjoy, and hopefully be inspired by what was done and salute, with me, the creative talents involved in designing the projects shown here and the photographers who have captured the accomplishments for us to experience.

Martin M. Pegler

Acknowledgements

My thanks to all the architects and designers who graciously provided not only the examples of their work but also the quotes that fill these pages. I have a long time relationship with many of these talented people and have relied on their talents in many of my previous books. For this book I have also made some new friends and I hope they will like how I have reported on their work.

The book would be lacking in color and definition if not for the photographers who provided the wonderful pictures that illuminate the text, so to one and all my sincerest appreciation and thanks.

To the people at Fairchild and Bloomsbury, my thanks for undertaking publishing a "picture book" in these perilous times and for doing it so beautifully. To the editors and artists and layout persons in New York and in England who worked on this book—THANK YOU!

A special thanks to my special "son", Jess Resnick, for diligently and painstakingly perusing the manuscript for errors I may have missed. He is probably the only person n the world who has actually read all of my books and not because he had to or because they were assigned reading.

To my children, my grandchildren and now my great-grandchildren—Laura, Molly, Jack and Charlotte; I am pleased to name you in my 80 something-eth book just as I named my children—Karen, Lysa and Adam in my first book and my grandchildren—Brian, Amanda, Jake, Sam, Ben and Marley—in recent books. A very special and proudly stated THANK YOU to Brian for the quote from his book that I used in the Introduction to this book.

And always—my love and thanks to Suzan, my wife, for creating and providing the safe and soft landing space for my "flights" into whatever moves me. She is the force behind my successes.

Martin M Pegler

PART 1

A Brand Is Born

CASE STUDIES

Sometimes it takes more than a set of parents to deliver a new brand; more than the clients who have conceived the new enterprise. Often it takes the architect or designer to serve as more than the midwife in the delivery. As the reader will soon discover as he or she peruses the brands in this section of the book, the creative designer's talent does play a major role in naming the "baby" and often in providing the "heritage" or backstory for the new brand.

According to the design team at Gruskin Architecture and Design that worked on the **Double Wide Grill**, the brand "is based on the imagined backstory that what was begun as a 1950s gas stop for travelers evolved into a restaurant." From that point on, the imagination of the design team was let loose to recreate the setting that now makes a dining experience at Double Wide Grill so memorable. **Sal Curioso**, as created by Stefano Tordiglione Design, is "madam's Spanish ex-lover and a world traveler who is curious and eccentric." So, based on this imaginary character, a dining experience was created using Mediterranean influences. As Stefano Tordiglione explains, "When a story is created, the deep discussion of brand positioning and identity has been established and then it is a step forward to make the theory a reality." **Youtopia** offers a whole new world for young shoppers to discover, while **Medi** attempts to simply bring the essence of a Greek fishing village into Arlington, Virginia.

We also have in this chapter "newborns" with names that are familiar but are now, for the first time, being introduced to the marketplace. **Vince Camuto**, globally known for his women's shoes, bags, and ready-to-wear, gets to open his first retail shop in which his several sub-brands are all represented. Located in the very busy Grand Central Terminal on East 42nd Street in New York City, the architects had several physical obstacles to overcome to create the desired ambience for the Camuto boutique.

Holt Renfrew, the well-established luxury Canadian department store, has created a new subdivision—**hr2**. The very elegant Canadian department store chain replaced their off-price brand, Last Call, with this new concept that is fresh and bright and delivers "great brands at value prices." A completely new and fashionable setting has been created for the new brand. Like Holt Renfrew, Barbisio has a long and illustrious heritage as a brand in Italy. The company wanted to create a new brand that would appeal to "the younger and trendier market of men and women." By adding the word "Factory" to the brand name, **Barbisio Factory** "maintains the visual cues (logo, graphics, naming) referring to the historical Barbisio but contemporarily declaring a new raising personality that is represented by experimentation, investigation, research in what is always fresh, new and distinctive." That called for a new brand identity—a new look for the retail setting.

PUMA, a very well established retail brand, opens a factory outlet center. This is new for the brand and calls for a new look, yet it has to maintain enough of the PUMA signature elements to satisfy the discount shopper that he or she is still buying the well-known brand.

For over 30 years, **être belle** makeup and body care products were only available in special boutiques and spas. Even though the products were available in almost 60 countries worldwide, there was no retail store that carried the whole product spectrum—until now. This is the first brick-and-mortar space designed for the brand and thus it joins our "born" brands. Already there are several siblings in the works.

Qela is an Arabian dream-fantasy of what a luxury boutique can look like when budget is no problem—and the effect is stunning. The brand features finely crafted leather goods, jewelry, and fashion, and the unique use of textures and luxurious materials creates an atmosphere of understated elegance and comfort. It is a refined gallery-like setting with touches of the Orient.

McCormick & Co. has a long and illustrious history as a brand but now—for the first time—opens its **World of Flavors** store and, as Joseph Bona of CBX (a brand agency specializing in corporate identity, consumer branding, and retail) explains, has the opportunity to highlight all of its products in a colorful space filled with the sights, sounds, and aromatic smells associated with cooking, baking, and grilling. In addition, since it is located at the Baltimore Harborside—a tourist-filled area—the store is filled with hands-on, fun activities as well as food tasting opportunities.

To introduce a new children's shoe store in Hong Kong, the design team at Stefano Tordiglione Design hit on "**apple & pie**" as the name and theme for the operation. As Stefano Tordiglione said, "the concept combines the well-being elements represented by the apple with the more playful pie." The combination added up to a whimsical, fresh approach that appeals to child and parent alike.

Though the owners of what is now **Susanna Pizzeria** were not new to the pizza business, this store was their entry into the US market. The brand name that flourished in Italy was not one that would easily slide off the American tongue, so the brand needed a name that would tie in with its Greenwich Village location as well as its Italian roots. The colors, textures, and general feel of the design and the use of their mother's name combine old with new and Italy with the United States.

Having designed a previous restaurant for the owners of **Central Kitchen**, the designers at Paxton Gate knew what was needed for this new space. They "served up a contemporary rustic look with an artisanal twist" and featured many recycled and reclaimed materials and elements to add the unique look that the brand demanded.

A new brand can be something totally new or it can be a sub-brand or a new venture for an established brand. Whatever or whoever its "parents" may be, the brand that has been born comes into the marketplace with a name, a countenance (logo), maybe a favorite color, and an appeal to the emotions and senses of its prospective "adopters" (customers).

CASE STUDY 1.1

DOUBLE WIDE GRILL

ADAM'S TOWNSHIP, PENNSYLVANIA, USA

DESIGN: GRUSKIN ARCHITECTURE + DESIGN P.C., SPRINGFIELD, NEW JERSEY, USA

DESIGN OBJECTIVE

Create the desired ambience and atmosphere for what was a 1950s vintage gas stop for travelers that evolved into a restaurant, as its operators began to serve food along with their gas sales. It all began with the imagined backstory conceived by Scott Kramer and Steve Zumoff, the owners of Double Wide Grill, and realized by Gruskin Group of Springfield, NJ. Speaking for the design team at Gruskin Group is Kenneth A. Gruskin, principal:

> *The brand sensibility includes a dose of kitschy sentiment that becomes some of the "campiness" of the dining experience. The goal is to communicate to the public that Double Wide is a place for good, down-to-earth "eats", where you can be yourself without pretense; a place where tradition combines with friend and family to meet for drinks, food, and good times hanging out together. The dining experience and environment captures the public's nostalgic fascination with "the open road" and "adventure travel" via the family car, trailer in tow.*

DESIGN SOLUTION

A dominant branding icon is the building itself; a building recognizable as a 1950s gas station (converted into a restaurant) with an authentic, gas station sourced interior. We incorporated authentic details from period gas stations like curved corner windows, old gas pumps on pump islands, two-toned painted brick and garage bay service doors. The interior also needed to remain gas station-industrial—almost raw—as if the proprietors figured they could turn their station into a restaurant by just placing some tables inside, but keeping the remainder as if it were an operating gas station. The new logo communicates the brand promise by bringing back the colors, styles and sentiment of the fifties gas station but in a contemporary manner. The bright yellow color "smiles at you," while the gas pump icon connects with the legacy of the brand. Gruskin explains, "The font is seemingly haphazard, reinforcing that Double Wide is the opposite of the other neighborhood chain restaurants—being more 'real' and 'authentic'."

Old gas station artifacts and found objects are used to create the ambience in the reception and take-out areas, and a rolling tool chest serves as a check-in for guests. Oil drums become displayers for the Double Wide collection of branded souvenirs and also act as counter-top supports. Gruskin continues: "Hubcaps decorate the ceiling, providing an interesting context in which the HVAC diffusers become just another circular metal object. Custom-made light fixtures fashioned from license plates, oil cans and car springs continue the garage theme. Dining booths incorporate car spring lights, gas pump nozzle wall accents, and a worn-in look that features old road signs, gas station memorabilia and gas station type materials." Reinforcing the humble beginnings of Double Wide are the concrete floors, open ceilings, painted block walls, and the exposed ductwork.

Details matter—and in the design of Double Wide Grill details fill the space and overflow it. In nice weather, five commercial garage doors can be opened so that diners may move out and dine al fresco on the front and rear decks. Or—for the more foolhardy—they can opt to dine under an old pick-up truck that has been hoisted up on a garage lift. Though colored lights illuminate the truck's underside, it does not obliterate the rusted carcass of the sagging truck. Three classic trailers complete the deck experience and diners may opt to actually dine in these icons of the open road.

How successful was this realization of the brand identity that was based on a backstory brand? The owners, Scott Kramer and Steve Zumoff, provide the answer. "The project has captured the essence of what we had hoped for when we invented the idea of the Double Wide Grill—it stands out from the other chain restaurants and authentically presents our vision of a gas station turned into a neighborhood bar and restaurant. In fact, the atmosphere and the brand are so authentic that many diners actually believe that Double Wide was a real gas station that was converted into a restaurant."

CONCLUSION

The effectiveness of the design is summed up by the awards the project has received. Selected by the International Council of Shopping Centers as the winner of the Silver award for Retail Design, the citation stated that Double Wide Grill's interior "has a worn-in look, and features old road signs, gas station converted memorabilia, old tires hung from the walls, lights made from car parts and trucks on lifts. It was designed to suggest a 1950s sensibility, while capturing the country's fascination with the open road." Double Wide Grill is thriving—and not on gas.

DESIGN CREDITS:

Design:	Gruskin Architecture + Design P.C., Springfield, New Jersey, USA Kenneth A. Gruskin, AIA: Design Joel Shulman, AIA: Project Leader
Clients:	Steve Zumoff and Scott Kramer of Double Wide Grill
Photography:	Kenneth A. Gruskin, Gruskin Architecture + Design P.C.

▲ **Figure 1:** It looks like the real thing—a 1950s garage/gas station—but is actually a new structure that serves as a restaurant filled with auto-related memorabilia. Two-toned painted brick and architectural details of the period make it seem authentic.

▶ **Figure 2:** The rolling tool chest serves as a check-in for guests in the reception and take-out area, which is decorated with gas station artifacts. Hubcaps fill the ceiling, adding to the garage look.

▶ **Figure 3:** The bar area and the main dining room have concrete floors, open ceilings, exposed ductwork, and painted block walls. Seen in the rear of the space is an ancient pick-up truck raised up on a lift.

▶ **Figure 4:** Guests can opt to dine under the rusty pick-up truck raised up on the garage lift. The underside of the lift is festooned with holiday lights that add a whimsical touch as well as point up the decrepit condition of the truck's underside.

◀ **Figure 5:** One of the booths in the dining room. Car springs serve as light fixtures while old signs, gas pump nozzles, and other found and reclaimed elements add to the overall early gas station/garage ambience.

▲ Figure 6: Three classic trailers of that bygone era are pulled up and embedded in the walls of the Double Wide Grill main dining area. Seen here, on the far right, is part of one that serves as a semi-private dining area for a small group.

▲ **Figure 7:** When the weather allows, the five commercial-style garage doors can be raised and dining can be moved out to allow an al fresco experience on the front and rear decks of the structure.

◀ **Figure 8:** The trailers as seen from outside the "garage." The front ends have "pierced" the corrugated metal exterior while the rear ends of the trailers are set up in some long-ago "trailer park" setting.

CASE STUDY 1.2

APPLE & PIE

ONE SOUTH ISLAND, HONG KONG, CHINA

DESIGN: STEFANO TORDIGLIONE DESIGN LTD., HONG KONG, CHINA

DESIGN OBJECTIVE

When two caring mothers, one originally from India (Shamsa Van Keulen) and the other from Austria (Anita Klaus), frustrated at not being able to find quality children's shoes in Hong Kong, decided to do something about it, they approached the Stefano Tordiglione Design firm for direction. Tordiglione explains what followed:

> *They were very courageous to set up this new company and in the beginning they were not sure about how to brand the new business. This is the moment that we stepped in: to create a concept. We believe it is important that we find out what the client wants and in this case the two business partners wanted to create a shop that would be fun for kids and at the same time provide shoes that fit and encourage the healthy growth of the young feet. This became the core value of the boutique.*

DESIGN SOLUTION

When working with a new client, Stefano Tordiglione, the Italian-born architect/designer based in Hong Kong, says: "It is essential that we ask the basic question: What is the value you wish to create? This is the foundation of the whole creation and with this—no matter if there is a previous brand identity or not—it is already a direction for the design concept and a step forward." The brand name "apple & pie," conceived by the two founders, and the logo that was developed by the designer, combines the healthy element associated with *apple* with the fun and playfulness of *pie*. Stefano Tordiglione explains: "The former is represented in the design concept by the use of environmentally and child-friendly materials with a focus on wood as opposed to plastic for the furnishings, while the 'playfulness' can be seen in the whimsical interior design." The logo elements—the apple and the pie—are both halved and combined into a single element that is introduced on the black wall of the façade. A giant outline of a red apple serves as a delightful demarcation for the entry into the store, which is almost completely visible through the great expanse of glass. The "pie"—represented by the half circle filled with a grid suggestive of the pastry strips that are often used to finish baked pies—appears up against the front glass and the open spaces are filled with featured shoes. According to the designer, "The semi-circular pie-like features bring the logo and brand name full circle while providing window shoppers with a taste of the various European shoe brands that can be found within." The same grid appears on the interior to provide a feature wall display.

Aside from the natural wood floor, the color palette plays up the red of the apples that appear throughout and the complementary green accents, all in a surround of crisp, clean white. Rounded and curved elements dominate and especially to be noted are the red apple-shaped poufs that serve as seating for parents and children alike. In a far corner is an area surrounded by a giant blackboard, where the children can "escape" to—to play or draw—between shoe fittings. A three-dimensional white "tree" becomes a focal element in the shop interior from which red and white apples are suspended. Though everything has been done to "make this a positive experience for the children," Tordiglione adds that the parents are not neglected: "The iconic Kartell chairs surrounding the low table, the Ethel lighting hanging from the ceiling above, and the giant red lamp designed by Anglepoise are design features that lend a sophisticated and elegant air to the store."

CONCLUSION

"Playfulness, elegance, and practicality come together" in this new brand—apple & pie Children's Shoe Boutique—and children can "enjoy choosing shoes that are displayed in a fun and enticing way in cheerful, relaxed surroundings." Once the clients are ready, the concept is ready for rollout with a memorable name and a recognizable logo—and its core value intact.

DESIGN CREDITS:

Store and Logo Design:	Stefano Tordiglione Design Ltd., Hong Kong, China Stefano Tordiglione: Chief Designer
Clients:	Anita Klaus and Shamsa Van Keulen
Construction:	Anzac
Lighting:	Ethel and Anglepoise
Furniture:	Kartell
Photography:	Courtesy of Stefano Tordiglione Design Ltd., Hong Kong, China

▲ **Figure 1:** The healthy quality of *apple* is combined with the fun of *pie* in this new children's shoe store. These signature elements appear prominently on the façade that wraps around the store's corner location. Note the apple-shaped entrance.

▲ **Figure 2:** The first impression of the interior is the color palette of white, red, and green complemented by the light, natural wood. Environmentally and child-friendly materials are used, with the focus on wood rather than plastics.

▲ **Figure 3:** Apple-shaped poufs covered in signature red fabric provide the seating while assorted-size white cylinders serve as display platforms. Rounded and curved forms predominate throughout the shop.

▲ **Figure 4:** The focal element in the shop is the whimsical white apple tree that is the feature displayer with highlighted red apples and the newest shoes on view in some of the white apples.

◀ Figure 5:
A child's play/activity area is located in the rear of the space and is surrounded by a giant blackboard upon which the children can draw or write. Children can "escape" to this place between fittings and have some fun.

▲ Figure 6: The view from the children's corner. The wall display fixtures are reminders of the "pie" in the store name along with the semi-circular forms shown in the open window areas. The grid plays up the pie-crust texture.

CASE STUDY 1.3

YOUTOPIA

RAVENSBURG, GERMANY

DESIGN: DAN PEARLMAN MARKENARCHITEKTUR GMBH, BERLIN

DESIGN OBJECTIVE

Create a fun environment for a new brand in an old building; an existing four-story building on Marienplatz in the town of Ravensburg. Youtopia was developed for and by the Bredl fashion group in conjunction with the dan pearlman Markenarchitektur design firm of Berlin. The store, which is 10,700 sq. ft, is a fashion world for fun-loving, young shoppers and filled with brands already popular with this group as well as casual leisurewear and hip party clothes. According to the PR material, it "appeals to young tastes with a Youtopia manifesto—its own language and matching look and feel." The manifesto is: "We are YOUnited in beYOUtiful YOUphOria!"

Volker Katschinski is the Creative Director Retail as well as a founder and Associate of the dan pearlman architectural design firm, and this is how he describes the Youtopia brand:

> *Youtopia—a place for dreams and where anything is possible. A fantasy world for presenting fashion innovatively and whisking customers away on a voyage of discovery. For the very first time, the team at dan pearlman took a fictional idea and transformed an entire four-story department store into a bona fide adventure. This also meant implementing a uniform concept that would allow for a range of distinct sales areas.*

DESIGN SOLUTION

Making the actual space vibrate with the brand concept meant using color, line, and visually stimulating cues. Katschinski explains: "The design and architecture of the store captivates shoppers with dazzling, colorful accents of paint dabs, tape designs, and street art elements throughout the retail space. From the broad black stripes painted in the stairwell, to the Youtopia manifesto displayed at the registers, to the old work bench display table and changing rooms with hooks fashioned from high heels—detail-rich elements transform shopping into an experience and inspire thirst for discovery."

Each of the four floors has a special fashion theme. Starting with the basement, Queen's Glamour offers glitz and chic wear while the street level—Queen's Casual—is where the shopper will find women's casual leisurewear. The next two floors are Queen's & King's Sport and King's Casual. Katschinski explains: "The concept not only pokes fun at fashion statements but also emphasizes an overall zest for life. Accordingly, the individual areas or shops-within-the-shop have names like Sparkling Jungle, Jungle Junction or Brave New Brainiac." A Youtopia banana, anyone? Visit Banana Island. Tying this urban jungle theme together and serving as its mascot/logo is the monkey, and monkeys seem to appear everywhere in the store. They are most evident in the Monkey Lounge, which promises to be the popular meeting place for the young, trendy shoppers of Ravensburg. Also, as an appeal to today's social media, so beloved by their target market, shoppers can photograph their favorite new item in the Photopia photo box and post it on the Youtopia Facebook page.

CONCLUSION

The transformation of the store for the Bredl fashion house was accomplished with a great awareness of tradition and geared exclusively at the young local "fashionistas" in this city of 50,000 residents. Proving that the parent company has "its finger on the pulse of time," Youtopia has been an immediate success. Volker Katschinski adds, "The decision to go for an international English concept instead of a purely Swabian-German one was a fully conscious choice since it then allows Ravensburg to serve as the point from which the brand can expand globally."

DESIGN CREDITS:

Design:	dan pearlman Markenarchitektur GmbH, Berlin
	Volker Katschinski: Creative Director Retail
	Jork Andre Dieter: Creative Director Visual Communications
	Sebastian Lange: Architecture
	Ayla Schilp: Art Director
	Diana Kaufmann: PR
Client:	Youtopia / Bredl Ravensburg
	Gerhard Gieseke: CEO Youtopia & Bredl
	Ivon Kanja: Store Manager, Youtopia
Photography:	Guido Leifhelm

◀ **Figure 1:** Once you leave the charming ancient square and enter the charming, century-old building you are in the world of Youtopia. It is a land for the young, the trendy, and the fun-loving.

▲ **Figure 2:** Monkey shines and monkey faces and bodies take over in the dark-hued realm of Youtopia. Mannequins wear monkey face masks and merchandise is displayed to attract the young shoppers. The four-story store is made up of different "worlds" for young men and women.

◀ **Figure 3:** Banana Island is one of those "worlds" and fits in with the monkey theme. The black, gray and yellow palette is carried through the store and helps accentuate the brightly colored merchandise.

◀ **Figure 4:** English is "spoken" here even though the "here" is in Germany. The management opted for English so that this design concept could "serve as a point from which to expand globally." Note the monkey and "we are YOUnited in beYOUtifUl YOUphOria."

◀ **Figure 5:** Brave New Brainiac is another "world." Drips and dabs of paint, street art, and controlled graffiti appear throughout the store along with elements of travel and movement.

◀ **Figure 6:** In this young men's shop the taped floor pattern and the assorted automobile tires add to the sense of movement and on-the-go. Though the visual merchandising is neat and sharp, there is a relaxed, "let-it-all-hang-out" quality to the shop.

◀ **Figure 7:**
The theme continues in Men's Shoes where Rolling Tapes is combined with a gorilla taking off in a yellow banana. Note the follow-through of unrolling tapes off the column on the right.

◀ **Figure 8:**
With monkeys and bananas everywhere it was natural to find the Jungle Junction next to the Monkey Lounge where shoppers can relax and enjoy the fun scene including the seating provided by the old truck.

CASE STUDY 1.4

SUSANNA PIZZERIA

BLEECKER STREET, GREENWICH VILLAGE, NEW YORK CITY, USA

DESIGN: SERGIO MANNINO STUDIO, BROOKLYN, NEW YORK CITY, USA

DESIGN OBJECTIVE

The pizzeria businesses that three brothers had established and been successful with near Verona, in Italy, needed a new look and design if the dream of Christian, Thomas, and Matteo was to have a chance in New York City. Their reputation for producing a high quality thin pizza was well known and their restaurants, Il Giglio, were beacons for pizza lovers in Italy. The collective dream was to come to New York, start a new life and open a pizzeria in the heart of Greenwich Village on Bleecker Street. After all—as the Kander and Ebb song goes—"If you can make it there, you can make it anywhere—New York—New York."

DESIGN SOLUTION

The Sergio Mannino Studio, in Brooklyn, New York, is a collective of creative professionals with roots in Italian design and culture, so it was a natural thing for the brothers to commission Sergio Mannino to design the new restaurant. This project was one of creating the brand identity for a new business based on an established brand—but moved to a new country and culture. Mannino says:

> *We wanted to create a modern space with a traditional feel. Their product is "familiar but very different" than the typical pizza you can find in New York. The thin crust they're known for is completely different from the Neapolitan pizza we have seen flourishing in the past few years, and is also different from the traditional Italian-American style that probably came from Sicily at the beginning of the twentieth century. The space we designed reflects the new approach while keeping a familiar feel to the space.*

However, the first problem, as Sergio Mannino saw it, was the name. Il Giglio (the lily flower) may have worked in Italy where Italians knew what the name meant and pronouncing it was not a problem, but since this was a new business in a new place, Mannino suggested a new, more readily pronounceable name. Susanna, their mother's name, was a unanimous choice and "we built the new identity with a new name and a reference to their original locations (in Italy)."

Taking center stage in the typical Greenwich Village ground floor store space are the kitchen and the pizza oven—enclosed in a dark area facing the restaurant and highlighted by a light-colored wooden counter. "The walls on each side of the restaurant evoke the spirit on which the concept of the space is based. On the left wall, the ceramic red and white tiles recall the domestic warmth of the traditional Italian kitchen and the familiar red-and-white checkered tablecloth. On the right, the exposed brick wall—characteristic of old New York—becomes the canvas for an original, fun and modern concept piece," adds Mannino, who also designed the artwork. The white chairs repeat the white of the brick wall and the hanging lights that also suggest a time gone by, and "draw the eye from the brightness of the ceramic tiles to the darkness of the ceiling and then to the open space in the rear of the restaurant leading out to the garden."

The metropolitan environment is captured in the outdoor dining area of the garden. Here, too, we see the Italian tradition of al fresco dining brought into the concept and recalling the original brand. Mannino explains: "The soft candlelight invites you into a garden space filled with wooden benches, a white painted fence, black metal tables and red plastic chairs." Adding to the flavor of the scene and to the senses are the plants out here that include basil, rosemary, oregano, and "other herbs and spices that provide the aromas of traditional Italian cuisine."

CONCLUSION

The design is a harmonious blend of traditional materials such as wood and ceramics used in conjunction with custom-designed furniture and fun graffiti. Sergio Mannino concludes: "Our aim was to design a space that would create contrasting yet coherent emotions. The result is a space driven by our passion to create something new—where Italian design meets the influence of metropolitan modernity." Though it was not a primary consideration for the design, the team at Sergio Mannino did plan for the inevitability of Susanna Pizzeria becoming a chain of pizzerias and thus the concept is readily adapted to a rollout in the future.

DESIGN CREDITS:

Design:	Sergio Mannino Studio, Brooklyn, New York City, USA
	S. Mannino , G. Bortolotti, G. Delpiano, L. Leone, G. Zuffanti
Client:	Susanna Pizzeria
Photography:	Edmon Leong. Courtesy of Sergio Mannino Studio

▶ **Figure 1:** The challenge was to introduce an Italian product to an American audience familiar with pizzas and show that this was something special. This had to look like a pizzeria that was different.

◀ **Figure 2:** As seen from the rear of the long and narrow space, the all-important ovens and counters are at the front and dining is set up beyond them. The color scheme is basically red, white, and black.

▶ **Figure 3:**
One wall is covered with red and white ceramic tiles to suggest the traditional checkered cloths used in rustic Italian restaurants. The chairs are white and tabletops natural wood.

▶ **Figure 4:** The opposite wall is brick that is painted white and a red line "graffiti" design is applied over it. The brick wall is a "typical" SoHo, NYC touch.

▶ **Figure 5:** The Italian love for al fresco dining is seen in the outdoor dining area where red chairs and black tabletops continue the color scheme, surrounded by a white fence.

CASE STUDY 1.5

SAL CURIOSO

WYNDHAM STREET, HONG KONG, CHINA

DESIGN: STEFANO TORDIGLIONE DESIGN LTD., HONG KONG, CHINA

DESIGN OBJECTIVE

To create the setting and place for a Madam Sixty Ate's ex-lover—Sal Curioso. She is the imaginary proprietress of a restaurant in Wanchai and the brainchild of Chris Woodyard and Bronwyn Cheung of Wooly Pig Concepts. Sal Curioso was to be the next restaurant in their domain. Stefano Tordiglione, the Italian-born, Hong Kong-located architect/designer was called upon to create the new space. Tordiglione explains: "While Madam is a feminine journeyer of other worlds, Sal Curioso is the Madam's Spanish ex-lover and a world traveler who is curious and eccentric. He is crazy about food and is a genius inventor of food machines." That was the backstory and the emphasis in the restaurant was to be on seafood and the Mediterranean Sea. "When a logo or story is created, the deep discussion of the brand positioning and identity has been established and then it is a step forward to make the theory a reality," says Tordiglione.

DESIGN SOLUTION

"A brand must be recognized through the design of the 'box' that contains the product. By 'box' I mean that shop or whatever it is that is designed to support the product. Furthermore, the major responsibility is to design something outstanding—but never too much—as the design must never overpower or overshadow the product. It is important to be honest in the creative process. By honest, I mean respectful of the product, of the DNA of the brand, and with these two things we have set thousands of ideas floating," said Stefano Tordiglione. Based on these imaginary characters, the design team created an atmosphere filled with Mediterranean influences. They sliced the space through the middle to create a distinct split "centered about a construct/deconstruct concept." "The middle section of the space is accentuated with sophisticated and elegant blue molded panels to create the sensation of floating for diners." The top and bottom, where cement, a neutral material, was used "reflects the imagination and ideas of the Spanish adventurer, Sal Curioso, while the middle zone, where the diners sit, is where his creations become a reality as diners consume Spanish fare. The contrast of gritty, contemporary concrete with classic paneling gives the dining area a luxurious feel."

Each area in the restaurant has its own, unique design. Inspired by the clubs of the 1970s, the lounge is "a welcoming cozy space" with optical wallpaper, colorfully upholstered sofas and red and black bar stools. Tordiglione explains:

> *Quirky and bright design themes continue throughout. From the bold, cut Spanish tiles of the bar—in keeping with the overriding construct/deconstruct concept—and inspired by the Spanish architect Gaudi's decoration, to the mixed-era furniture including fifties chairs and sixties banquettes we designed especially, and seventies vintage lamps on the chef's table, the restaurant is a delightful gallimaufry [hodge-podge] of eras and worlds that come together under one roof.*

Throughout, the designer added unique details to suggest Sal Curioso's voyages, like the wave-like, sandblasted mirrors that surround the sleek, stainless steel open kitchen that are not only reminiscent of ocean travel but the importance of seafood in the Mediterranean cuisine. The patterns and prints that decorate the large, centrally located columns are inspired by the Alhambra, in Spain.

CONCLUSION

According to Stefano Tordiglione, "The aim of all these designs is to create the brand identity of the restaurant and to give it a soul. In a diner's heaven such as Hong Kong, the restaurant business is very competitive and it is very important to build up a unique brand to distinguish oneself from all the others." Sal Curioso has taken its place in the Hong Kong restaurant hierarchy.

DESIGN CREDITS:

Design:	Stefano Tordiglione Design Ltd., Hong Kong, China
	Stefano Tordiglione: Chief Designer
Client:	Wooly Pig Concepts
	Chris Woodyard and Bronwyn Cheung
Contractor:	NYC Renovations
Photography:	Stefano Tordiglione Design Ltd., Hong Kong, China

▶ Figure 1:

The restaurant was created around the concept of a curious and eccentric world traveler who loved good food and was the inventor of food machines.

◀ **Figure 2:** "Centered about a construct/ deconstruct concept," the middle section is highlighted with elegant blue molded panels to suggest the sensation of "floating in space."

◀ **Figure 3:** The patterns on the columns are inspired by motifs found in the Alhambra in Spain. The contrast of gritty, contemporary concrete with classic paneling and fine materials gives the eating zone a luxurious feel.

▶ **Figure 4:** Inspired by the architect Gaudi, there are cut Spanish tiles at the bar—"in keeping with the construct/ deconstruct concept"—as well as a mixture of furniture from different eras.

▶ **Figure 5:** Throughout, there are references to Sal Curioso's voyages with the use of wave-like patterns such as those seen on the back wall and in more detail in Figure 1.

CASE STUDY 1.6

CENTRAL KITCHEN

SAN FRANCISCO, CALIFORNIA, USA

DESIGN: PAXTON GATE DESIGN/BUILD, SAN FRANCISCO, CALIFORNIA, USA

DESIGN OBJECTIVE

The Ne Timeas Restaurant group, also known as Thomas McNaughton, David Steele, and David White, decided to open their new restaurant in a converted industrial building in San Francisco's Mission District that would pay homage to Northern California cuisine. The new restaurant, Central Kitchen, would also feature a retail shop and a salumeria. In addition to creating the look and feel of the new place—creating the brand identity—"driving the new design was the challenge of providing outdoor dining that feels perfect when it is nice out, and still perfect when the weather turns moody."

What appealed to the young restaurateurs about Paxton Gate, the San Francisco based design firm, under the leadership of Sean Quigley and Todd McCrea, was that it has "an accessible aesthetic based on the natural sciences and has as its mantra the three 'Rs': refurbished, repurposed, reclaimed." It was only reasonable that the trio would call upon Paxton Gate when they required a design that was clean and modern and would work in the industrial location.

DESIGN SOLUTION

For the Paxton Gate team, it was finding a way "to address the Northern California menu by creating elements that reflected our interpretations of the topography, and the flora and fauna of the region. We also felt that there needed to be a connection to Flour + Water (the restaurant previously designed by Paxton Gate for the Ne Timeas restaurant group) in some way. We wanted an airy space that reflected what we love about the postmodernism that came out of Northern California, but had a more industrial edge to it." Todd McCrea explains: "We chose materials that were industrial in nature, oftentimes repurposing them from their original intent. We selected steel sheets, I-beam, and angle iron and paired them with walnut and redwood. We acid stained the concrete floors with a warmer color that supported an earthy base to the design." As they did in Flour + Water, "we added beams to humanize the scale of the space and create a rhythm that would break the space into units rather than one, big open space. We added reclaimed I-beams to achieve this." Since the outdoor dining element was so important, and from the entrance the diner enters into the courtyard with seating for 30 guests, "these beams extended into the courtyard to create a cohesive space, rather than an inside and outside room. The beams also embraced the history of the site—embracing its industrial past. The covering to the courtyard 'floats' above the space to allow maximum light to enter the space, while allowing it to be watertight and comfortable." The custom-designed retractable roof/awning combination allows for outdoor dining no matter what the weather may be.

To create the look and feel that is the Central Kitchen brand, many reclaimed and repurposed elements went into the overall design—like the school gym floor, from a school that no longer exists, that became the ceiling of the salumeria. A centerpiece of the outdoor dining room is the water feature with a cast iron pipe flange framed by redwood and raw steel. It is illuminated from both sides from behind acrylic panels and stretched steel. Hardie boards—cement fiberboards—were used on the walls of the interior room since they are "an industrial, cost effective and readily available material." "They were painted with three different colors that represented the surrounding hills, and arranged in a Mondrian-esque pattern. Earthy walnut was used on all of the furniture to ground the design and give it a warm base." Adding another unique element to the design was the use of the ancient Japanese practice of burnt wood on the siding.

CONCLUSION

"What we try to do is create an experience that resonates with people. Our approach is much more like an installation artist. This doesn't imply that we think we are artists, but we want people to feel things when they enter a place we design. Many materials have a psychological connection to them and may cause people to feel or remember something from their own lives. The beauty in this is that the person sitting at the table next to you can have a totally different experience because of how the space makes them feel, or what it causes them to remember. Similarly, installation art provides a space to enter, with deliberate decisions made, but it's still left to the viewer to fill in the blanks. The trick is to create a space that also supports the goals of the clients or owners so that there is always an underlying consistency that supports their vision"—and their brand.

DESIGN CREDITS:

Design:	Paxton Gate Design/Build, San Francisco, California, USA Todd McCrea and Sean Quigley: Designers
Client:	Ne Timeas Restaurant Group: Thomas McNaughton, David Steele, and David White
Photography:	César Rubio

◀ **Figure 1:** Located in a converted industrial building in San Francisco, Central Kitchen has as its mantra: refurbished, repurposed, and reclaimed. The entrance is through the courtyard, which has seating for 30 guests.

◀ **Figure 2:** The covering in the courtyard floats above the space and the retractable roof/awning allows outdoor dining in all sorts of weather. The reclaimed I-beams that extend out from the dining room create a cohesive space.

◀ **Figure 3:** The repurposed beams humanize the scale of the space and also refer to the space's industrial heritage. Steel sheets, I-beams, and angle irons are combined with maple and redwood while the acid-stained concrete floors provide "an earthy base to the design."

▶ **Figure 4:** To complement the Northern California menu the designers created elements that suggested the topography and natural elements of the area. Though many materials were industrial in nature, they were repurposed in this design.

▶ **Figure 5:** A retail shop and Italian salumeria are part of Central Kitchen and carry the brand's identity in the materials used. Rough textured walls and factory windows add to the industrial feel.

◀ **Figure 6:** What was once the floor of a now razed school is the ceiling seen here. Adding a homey quality to this area are the walnut fixtures and the warm lighting that also enhance the look of the Italian-style food shop.

CASE STUDY 1.7

QELA

THE PEARL, DOHA, QATAR

DESIGN: UXUS, AMSTERDAM, THE NETHERLANDS

DESIGN OBJECTIVE

The Qatar Luxury Group was looking for a groundbreaking retail experience that would introduce their new global luxury brand—Qela. The Qela collection of women's fashion, leather goods, and jewelry are designed and crafted in Qatar to the highest standards. On the company's website it speaks of Qela being "warm winds tirelessly imposing fleeting patterns on the dunes—the rustle of the veil—a yearning for a future of shared cultures—a rich ornamental door laced with copper." "Qela speaks of fashion, but also of the history of generations from which it emerged. Qela encapsulates the dream of the traveler, the coincidence born of ancient traditions and the contemporary vision of a free spirit open to art and different cultures."

According to Oliver Michell, the Chief Creative Officer/Architect of UXUS, the global strategic design consultancy which was awarded the contract for developing Qela's global retail platform, "The Qela experience has its roots in travel and embodies its native country's aesthetics of quiet, pure and natural landscapes."

DESIGN SOLUTION

Based on the statements above, Oliver Michell continues:

> *Undulating forms and flowing curves echo majestic Qatari vistas, punctuated with rich, luxurious materials and a palette of elegant desert tones to highlight the Qela collection. The unique use of textures and branded design elements convey an atmosphere of understated elegance and comfort that is iconic to Qela. Bronze, solid walnut, travertine and distinctive* nero d'avola *stone slabs are softened by bespoke hand-knotted silk rugs and swaths of satin and linen curtains.*
>
> *Celebrating the brand's Arabic roots, the store features a signature Qela moucharabieh (latticework screen) pattern created from distinct elements of the Qela logo. The pattern forms the façade and, through free-standing moucharabieh bronze screens inspired by abstract dhow sails, defines intimately curated spaces within the store. Around the upper floor, individualized*

services and made-to-measure couture collections immerse clients in a tailored shopping experience. At the heart of this personal experience, the cashmere-tented Private Salon draws inspiration from the hospitality of desert hearths and invites customers to enjoy a moment of calm.

The store strikes a delicate balance between the brand's cultural heritage and its progressive spirit—immersing customers in the world of art, culture, and design. Following this concept, the boutique's design blends the atmosphere of an intimate salon with the dynamism of a world-class art space: inviting clients to explore a continuously changing gallery of crafted luxury products and fine art.

To accomplish this, product displays are focused on solid wood and stone pedestals or plinths and the walls are reserved for the hanging or projection of artwork. Muted tones of tan, dove-gray, and blush "embody local identity with references to Arabic culture and the Gulf's landscape." Cutting-edge low-energy lighting can be remotely positioned and dimmed to bring out the inherent qualities in the works of art or the luxury products being presented. Also, rather than traditional window displays, shoppers are greeted by video programming of the art being shown within the boutique.

CONCLUSION

Oliver Michell says: "At the intersection of culture, fashion and design, Qela represents the twenty-first-century definition of luxury as the ultimate blend of art, savoir-faire, and innovation. The new retail experience embodies these brand qualities, taking customers on an aspirational journey that sets a new benchmark for the world of luxury."

DESIGN CREDITS:

Design:	UXUS, Amsterdam, The Netherlands Oliver Michell: Chief Creative Officer/Architect
Client:	Qatar Luxury Group Caroline Guillon: VP, Marketing & PR Vincent Ragot: VP, Retail Division Maelle Foucault: Visual Merchandising Manager Gregory Couillard: CEO
Contractor:	LEAD Construction
Fixture Manufacturer:	The Set Company
Lighting:	DPA Lighting / RCL Lighting
Photography:	Adrian Haddad

▲ **Figure 1:** The Qela experience starts with promotional material for gallery-like showings of artists and native craftspeople.

◀ **Figure 2:** Upon entering the dramatic, two-story space, the shopper is immediately immersed in a feeling of luxury and splendor.

▲ Figure 3:
On ground level, the fine leather goods are displayed like precious artwork atop wood or stone plinths while paintings adorn the walls as in a gallery.

▶ Figure 4:
In keeping with the desert tones and Arabic influences, a majestic staircase curves and sweeps up to the upper level of the shop.

◀ **Figure 5:** Rounded, voluptuous couches overloaded with pillows and satin draperies along the walls all add softening elements to the dramatic architecture of the space.

▶ **Figure 6:** Around the upper level there are individualized services and couture collections to behold. Abstract mannequins on pedestals, like sculptures in a museum, show off featured garments. Offering Arabic hospitality is the fire in the hearth on the second level.

◀ **Figure 7:** Throughout, bronze moucharabieh screens—with elements of the Qela logo—unfurl like the sails of the local dhows.

◀ **Figure 8:** The private salon "draws inspiration from the hospitality symbolized by desert hearths and invites customers to enjoy a moment of calm."

CASE STUDY 1.8

MEDI

ARLINGTON, VIRGINIA, USA

DESIGN: GRIZFORM DESIGN ARCHITECTS, WASHINGTON, DC, USA

DESIGN OBJECTIVE

Create a pleasant and pleasing setting for a new and modern quick-service, Greek restaurant in an aged building with a dated façade. Taking cues from the client's Greek background for the design, the concept should capture "the Old World charm of the Mediterranean in a fresh and modern way by balancing rustic and contemporary design."

DESIGN SOLUTION

When Griz Dwight, Principal and Owner of GrizForm Design Architects of Washington, DC was asked, "How much information do you get about the brand before you can design the space?"—this was his reply: "It really depends upon the project. Some projects begin with a very clear direction of where to go, but others are wide open and it's up to us to develop the language that colors the brand. We often seek out the projects which are very loose and very open in terms of brand and look. We like to get involved on the ground level and work up from there."

Griz Dwight and his team had that opportunity offered to them when they accepted the challenge of creating Medi, a 40-seat restaurant serving Greek food in the Shirlington neighborhood of Arlington, Virginia. According to Griz Dwight, "The space is housed in an aged building where most of the retail tenants have aged—along with dated awnings above entryways." He explains:

> *We did quite a bit of studying. We looked at other brands in the same sector; we looked at the store for historical references. We looked at the immediate neighborhood to see what is there and what may be lacking and we looked for inspiration completely outside the brand. I think that sometimes the freshest looks are those derived from something completely unexpected.*

The entry design was of prime importance to both the client and the design team as a necessary step into the neighborhood and into the store's interior. The façade was resurfaced with white stucco and marble and the striking and emphatic blue door, flanked by large glazed areas, became "the icon of Greek coastal towns and also part of the Medi logo." With a small floor area, Griz Dwight incorporated a color palette of whites and blues to help open up the interior space. To create the modern, yet vintage-inspired, look for Medi, the left side wall carries through the blue color introduced outside while the opposite wall is white marble with a dramatic band of blue—running the length of the store—that carries the store name/logo. These are complemented by an unfinished concrete floor that "helps balance the rustic yet contemporary look." To counteract the long space, oak beams traverse the ceiling and carry the custom lighting fixtures wrapped in heavy hemp rope that "were inspired by the elements and shapes you find at the fishing docks. Their placement also helped to visually break up the long, narrow space," says Dwight. The oak beams, wood-paneled areas, and the table tops in the dining area add "warmth to the coolness of the marble." The nautical theme is continued by a series of vintage pulleys, suspended from the ceiling by rope, that separate the five framed black and white photographs on the signature blue wall.

CONCLUSION

"I think the designer needs to bring something that is visually recognizable and unique. You don't want customers to confuse one store with another," says Griz Dwight. That doesn't happen in Arlington, where the iconic blue door at Medi makes its opening statement and carries through with its promise of "Old World charm of the Mediterranean in a fresh and modern way."

DESIGN CREDITS:

Design:	GrizForm Design Architects, Washington, DC, USA
	Griz Dwight: Principal and Owner
	Michelle Bove: Architect
	Brooke Loewen: Lead Interior Designer
Client:	Medi
Contractor:	Winmar Construction
Millwork:	Phoenix Woodworking
Photography:	Paul Burk Photography

◀ **Figure 1:** The refinished façade of white stucco, marble, and a signature blue suggested that the neighborhood had a new and friendly Greek dining experience. Medi offers "Old World charm of the Mediterranean in a fresh and modern way."

▼ **Figure 2:** The palette of white and blue helps to open up the rather small space, with one long wall painted the blue color introduced on the exterior and white marble on the facing wall.

◀ **Figure 3:** The blue wall is enhanced by five framed pictures of Greek fishing village scenes, and the nautical theme is continued by the vintage pulleys suspended by rope from the ceiling.

◀ **Figure 4:** The oak beams that stretch across the narrow store and the wooden seats and table tops add warmth to the cool surfaces, while the concrete floor "helps balance the rustic yet contemporary look."

▶ Figure 5: A closer look at the nautical elements like the rope-wrapped light fixtures, the antique pulleys, and the framed pictures. Together, these elements subtly add to the Greek flavor of the Medi design.

CASE STUDY 1.9

McCORMICK WORLD OF FLAVORS

HARBORPLACE, LIGHT STREET PAVILION, BALTIMORE, MARYLAND, USA

DESIGN: JGA, SOUTHFIELD, MICHIGAN, USA

DESIGN OBJECTIVE

It is not a surprise that McCormick's 3818 sq. ft space in Baltimore's Harborplace Light Street Pavilion is called McCormick World of Flavors since McCormick is a global leader in flavor. The company, under various brand names, manufactures, markets, and distributes spices, seasoning mixes, and condiments throughout the world. The architectural design firm JGA of Southfield, Michigan was commissioned "to create an experiential showcase featuring McCormick global leadership in flavor through three platforms: cooking, baking and grilling." This would be the company's first branded retail destination and would allow visitors to interact with some of the McCormick brands like OLD BAY®, Zatarain's®, Thai Kitchen®, and Grill Mates®.

DESIGN SOLUTION

Signature McCormick identity elements begin on the store's façade. There is the McCormick brand block that extends into the center with a "flavor band" and Duratrans signage that offers a view into the shop's interior. The loft-like interior is reminiscent of the McCormick plant and headquarters that existed nearby from 1920 to 1989. It was important that this space serve not only as a corporate brand showcase but further identify with McCormick's roots in Baltimore. The store is organized by a series of zones focusing on branding in key product categories and activity areas. In addition to cooking demonstrations and product sampling there are assorted activities and digital experiences for visitors to enjoy. The barbecue area resembles a dream back yard set-up where the Grill Mates products are featured with the natural light adding to the outdoor feel. Experiential moments are showcased in vignettes and the familiar red caps that cover the McCormick spice/herb bottles become giant brand signature elements clustered in the Red Cap alcove and as a canopy to highlight areas. There is also a history wall that proudly presents the company's heritage and tradition.

Ken Nisch, Chairman and Project Principal of JGA explains: "McCormick was focused on the concept of flavor—a portfolio of flavors supported by a series of things such as demonstration kitchen, interactive—all which reinforce the flavor positioning, while recognizing the distinctive nature of each. Each of their brands is revered in their own genre as well as by those who appreciate the visual culinary heritage of each of these spaces and their cultural roots." To be truly effective in creating the brand identity the design should appeal to all the senses and Ken Nisch agrees:

> *Branding is 360 degrees. Today, branding starts before the customer comes to the store. There is the traditional advertising as it might have been done in the past—catalogs, newspaper ads, and such—and today there is also social networking like YouTube, Facebook, and blogs, and we get the opinions and influences of friends and family as well as thought leaders who comment about essentially every point of life. The sensory cues of aroma, music, tastings, displays, etc. can bring these opinions to life, but more importantly, they imbed these opinions beyond the front of the mind into the deeper emotional fabric of memory.*

He continues:

> *A key component is the personal touch. Shoppers who purchase online miss the emotional and sensory cues. We call this the "soft experience" and in this case it is easy as there is no more emotional or evocative category of retail than food as it is totally embedded with tradition and culture and memory. In this shop everything—from food demonstrations with the cultural heritage of each brand, the sampling that takes place, and even the "virtual sampling" through things like "Flavor Print" which allow people to connect and match recipes and flavors and spices—reinforces the sensory cues.*

In addition to the striking accent of the signature red of the red cap, the palette includes culinary-inspired finishes such as stainless steel, aluminum, marble, and natural wood. To further the loft-like appeal the polished concrete floors and open ceiling use the "bones" as a background element to contrast with the recycled, reclaimed wood that serves as tabletops. The red tile façade distinguishes the demo kitchen with its unique marble top.

In summing up this project Ken Nisch says: "This concept was created as more of an experiential base. It essentially becomes kind of a common ground for testing, prompting, and validating ideas. Its focus is on how to talk to this cross-section of influencers in a real world—in real time. It does so both explicitly in terms of soliciting consumers but, more importantly, implicitly through data gathering across five interactive developments that allow McCormick to measure consumer interests, areas of confusion, areas of opportunity—all through the 75% consumer usage of the store's interactive network."

CONCLUSION

"This project is really a portfolio of brands and within this portfolio are brands that are appropriate to different uses, occasions, adventures, and traditions. They promote the idea of experimentation, openness, and adventure with food. So the whole idea of the store basically says that they all carry the McCormick promise of quality, and they do so in a way that is unexpected and really takes you beyond your everyday pepper, cinnamon, etc., into cultures, cuisines, history, and combinations. The Experience Center/Store is designed to basically get people comfortable with the idea that all things within the McCormick brand umbrella are available to make your life more interesting, your friends happier, while creating new traditions of entertainment."

DESIGN CREDITS:

Design:	JGA, Southfield, Michigan, USA Ken Nisch: Chairman and Project Principal
Client:	McCormick Lori Robinson: VP, Corporate Branding & Communication
Retail Consultants:	Brand Theater: Frank Dinunzi and John Ariotta Bentz-Papson Associates: Rick Bentz
Interactive Exhibits:	5th Screen Digital Services: John Curran and Keith Kelsen
Specialty/ Theatrical Fixtures:	Blue Genie Art: Kevin Collins
Photography:	Laszlo Regos Photography, Berkley, Michigan, USA

◀ **Figure 1:** Shoppers at the Baltimore Harborplace readily recognize the McCormick block logo from the hundreds of McCormick spice packages they have purchased in the past. All that signature red color also reinforces the brand's appearance here.

▼ **Figure 2:** This is the brand's first retail destination and its loft-like design is reminiscent of the McCormick plant that was located nearby from 1920 to 1989.

▲ **Figure 3:** The red caps that cover McCormick spice jars appear in oversized form as a canopy over the Red Cap area up front. They highlight one of the many zones devoted to product categories or the interaction activity areas.

▶ **Figure 4:** To further the loft look, the polished concrete floors and open, industrial ceiling serve as a backbone for the concept, while recycled, reclaimed wood is used as tabletops. Complementing these materials are stainless steel, aluminum, and marble.

◀ **Figure 5:** Each of the several McCormick brands is "revered in their own genre as well as by those who appreciate the visual culinary heritage of each of these spaces and their cultural roots." And—there are also souvenir T-shirts and hats to remember the McCormick experience.

◀ **Figure 6:** "Sensory cues" are reinforced throughout the space whether by taste, smell, or sight. Interactive activities allow shoppers to match their taste buds and their knowledge in regard to all things "spice."

▶ **Figure 7:** Special McCormick red tiles are combined with gray marble for this tasting station. The barbecue area resembles a back yard set-up where Grill Mates products are featured.

▼ **Figure 8:** The demo kitchen is where cooking fills the space with spice-driven aromas and promises of tastings to come. Here the red tiles cover the front and are topped with a marble counter. Throughout, monitors enliven the area with product messages.

CASE STUDY 1.10

VINCE CAMUTO

GRAND CENTRAL TERMINAL, EAST 42ND STREET, NEW YORK CITY, USA

DESIGN: SERGIO MANNINO STUDIO, BROOKLYN, NY

DESIGN OBJECTIVE

This store in the Grand Central Terminal on East 42nd Street in Manhattan is the first retail space to show off the complete Vince Camuto brand of footwear, handbags, outerwear, and accessories. The Camuto Group has proven itself an industry leader for the design, development, and distribution of women's fashion footwear and other sub-brands, and the hallmarks of the Camuto Group are "superior quality of product, unsurpassed value and consistency of branding."

The design, created by the design team at Sergio Mannino Studio of Brooklyn under the leadership of Sergio Mannino, had to balance "modern product display elements with a sharp material palette to frame, reflect and layer Camuto's edgy feminine style."

DESIGN SOLUTION

The following is, according to Sergio Mannino, how the designers created that Vince Camuto brand identity:

When we approach a new project with a client we usually get a brief describing the brand, the average customer demographic, the brand's values and goals, and its direct competitors. Sometimes we are asked to redesign the store concept for an existing brand and in that case most of the information is already widely available and the customers are already familiar with a specific design. In this case the client might want to change a strategy that is not working as expected or to update and expand the brand to include different type of products or a wider audience. When we started working with Vince Camuto the brand had already been developed, even if it was still new, but they did not have any store. Vince wanted to create a space that looked fresh, sophisticated, and very elegant. It had to be designed for women who cannot afford to shop at Prada, Michael Kors, or Gucci but that at the same time wanted to feel unique and needed a product (shoes, handbags, or accessories) that is well designed and very well crafted but still affordable. We also wanted to design a unique look and feel for the space. The brand was fairly new and we needed to distinguish it from any of its competitors and also from the higher end brands. This is of course a general approach as we always do our best to create a design that is unique, new, and that reflects the spirit of our time.

Since we had already designed the Vince Camuto showroom, many of the same elements were implemented in the store design as well. It is important, when creating or updating the image of a brand, that you create elements that are easy to spot and recognize and that are not seen anywhere else. By generating a repetition of elements (including colors, finishes, logos etc.) people remember the brand and start connecting with it. The lighting, especially in retail, is probably the most important element of the design. You can create an amazing store but if the lighting is not adequate, or it doesn't render the colors as what they actually are, then the product will not display correctly. Clients today enter a store expecting to immerse themselves into the brand. They want to "feel" the brand with all their senses and be part of it. The lighting is a crucial part of this experience.

There were also structural challenges that the design team faced, like columns that blocked views and made it difficult to place the fixtures in the space. To counteract that, the team created a shelving system that wraps the column on the left side while connecting them on the right side.

CONCLUSION

White lacquer, polished chrome, and a ceramic floor along with the color palette that combines various shades of gray produced the desired balance of modernism with sophistication and created the ideal setting for the Vince Camuto brand.

DESIGN CREDITS:

Design:	Sergio Mannino Studio, Brooklyn, New York City, USA Sergio Mannino, Francesca Scalettaris, and Allesandra Prezzi
Client:	Vince Camuto
Photography:	Courtesy of Sergio Mannino

◀ **Figure 1:** One of the problems the architects faced in setting up this store in the Grand Central Terminal in New York City was that the floor level was higher than the rest of the terminal. The added height actually added stature to the interior design.

◀ **Figure 2:** By wrapping the columns on the left and connecting them on the right, the columns not only function as shelving fixtures but become decorative assets in the design concept.

▶ **Figure 3:** A closer look at the column treatment as a fixture and part of the architectural design.

◀ Figure 4:
"Lighting is a crucial part of the experience of getting the 'feel' of the brand." The illuminated wall adds to that "feel" while also highlighting the product display presented on the floating shelves.

◀ **Figure 5:** Mirrored walls, recessed niches for garments, and vertical illuminated columns to accentuate small accessory items all add to the distinctive modern look of the Vince Camuto shop. The palette of shades of gray offers "a balance of modernism and sophistication."

◀ **Figure 6:** The Mondrian-ish metal frame in front of the illuminated back wall is an effective way of bringing interest to an otherwise long run of shelves.

PUMA FACTORY OUTLET CENTER

CARLSBAD, CALIFORNIA, USA

ARCHITECTURE/DESIGN: COLKITT&CO, SAN DIEGO, CALIFORNIA, USA

DESIGN OBJECTIVE

Nathan Lee Colkitt, principal and CEO of Colkitt&Co, the architectural design firm based in San Diego, CA which was commissioned to carry out PUMA's vision for the design of the PUMA factory outlet store in Carlsbad, CA explains: "A brand like PUMA is very diverse and has various meanings for different people. For each brand you have to boil it down to its essence and parse it into a basic diagram that allows for the greatest amount of interaction and interpretation for everyone to explore and have fun." The team followed PUMA's vision on JOY, SUSTAINABILITY, and CREATIVITY as the essence of the PUMA brand and explain how these core values were adapted in the design: "From a construction, design, sustainability, and investment perspective all branding elements were purposely selected to improve shopability for the customer and foster a better lifecycle of materials."

DESIGN SOLUTION

Colkitt said that they worked closely with the PUMA group: "We always start with the operations side of any brand with the understanding that you need operations, design, and creative merchandise to balance any space. We develop all retail concepts around a foreground, middle ground and background concept. The foreground is the merchandising such as the simple stands and props. The middle ground is the fixturization. This concept frames the product like a beautiful meal—nicely plated on a white tablecloth—allowing the merchandise to pop! The background is the architecture such as the walls, floor, and lighting which are all subservient and should drop back. From here we weave the branding at key moments in the customer experience with maximum impact, including the storefront, fitting rooms, and register. It all flows like a good story with a beginning, a middle, and an end—with the product as the hero and climax."

"We just exploded and disassociated the floor, walls, and ceiling, so the experience could be shaped by the customer and the product, not by the architecture. This allows for each customer to read into the space however they want. The branded elements are contained at the signature experiences such as the storefront, fitting rooms, and register, all with red corrugated metal and leaping cats." As for PUMA's vision of JOY, SUSTAINABILITY, and CREATIVITY:

> *JOY—inherent in both sports and life. The space is fun, quirky, and uplifting. You can hang in the heart of the store on the huge cushions and just daydream or joke with friends. If you prefer to get in and out more quickly, the style and size runs are logically organized to facilitate that.*
>
> *SUSTAINABILITY—create a safe and peaceful environment. From the clever little bag, to the bamboo, the recycled metals, modular furniture, basic pipes, LED lighting, and the simple methods of construction with just a socket set, the space is brimming with thoughtful choices relative not just to today, but to the future. The design concept is setting a precedent for LEED certified retail design in the outlet mall setting.*
>
> *CREATIVITY—expressing the individual in art and performance. The space is fun and interactive. All fixtures are mobile—including the fitting room— so that lends itself to interaction and change. You can come into the store and see a completely different layout each visit. All graphics are giant magnets that can be changed around overnight, as well as having custom artwork for different regions and campaigns.*

To enhance the look and feel of the space, there is the appeal to the senses. Colkitt notes that "PUMA is a product forward brand so sound, smell, and touch are huge. Natural textures were added such as real iron, bamboo, and recycled leather to contrast with the bright colors of the lifestyle gear. The sounds and smells are all product driven, and allow customers to shape their own relationship directly with the products. The strategy was to create a mid-ground fixturization of natural materials to 'support' the product first and put everything within arm's reach."

CONCLUSION

And, since according to Colkitt every good story should have a "happy ever after," the global reach of PUMA inspired the design model for this store to also be rolled out nationwide or even globally.

"Every culture is imbued with different habits and tendencies; however, good proportions are timeless. We thought out every material from the viewpoint of what is ubiquitous and available on every inhabited continent—some of which include hot rolled mild steel, iron pipe, corrugated metal, expanded metal, and plywood. This allows our fixtures to be fabricated regionally and take on regional connection details and modules. This provides a much more substantive and relevant relationship with locality rather than cliché moves like local motifs, graphics, and imagery."

DESIGN CREDITS

Architecture/ Design:	Colkitt&Co, San Diego, California, USA Nathan Lee Colkitt: Principal and CEO
Client:	PUMA North America
Photography:	Cheryl Ramsay, San Diego, CA

◀ **Figure 1:** "The branded elements are contained at the signature experience such as the storefront with red corrugated metal and leaping cats." The bright red window background sets the Puma look for the store.

▲ **Figure 2:** In the open, neutral colored space, the brand identity takes form in the signature red color that pops up throughout and in the use of sustainable materials that are part of the PUMA brand sensibility.

▲ **Figure 3:** Giant black poufs, covered in recycled leather and emblazoned with the leaping puma in red, serve as seating for trying on shoes or as a place "to hang out, just daydream or joke with friends."

▶ **Figure 4:** All fixtures are moveable—even the ones lining the perimeter walls. "You can come into the store and see a completely different layout each visit." It is part of what makes the space "fun and interactive."

▼ **Figure 5:** The fitting rooms—also moveable—are constructed of recycled corrugated metal with signature red curtains for privacy.

CASE STUDY 1.12

ÊTRE BELLE

FRANKFURT, GERMANY

DESIGN: BLOCHER BLOCHER SHOPS, STUTTGART, GERMANY

DESIGN OBJECTIVE

être belle is a privately owned company in Germany that for the past 30 years has been producing cosmetics and beauty aids. Known worldwide, être belle is synonymous with exclusive cosmetic and spa products including professional treatment systems. According to the company's website, "The main objective of être belle has always been to provide both beauticians and consumers—in nearly 60 countries worldwide—with high-quality, effective and skin-friendly cosmetic products. The products are made from natural ingredients, and presented in attractive and environmentally friendly packaging for the best value-for-money. The strategy is focused on growth, both in quantitative and qualitative terms."

As designed by Blocher Blocher Shops of Stuttgart, this store in Frankfurt is the company's first brick-and-mortar appearance for the brand. Angela Kreutz, Head of Communications at the design firm explains: "This gave us freedom in the design process because there was no predecessor. Before this premiere, the company mainly distributed its assortment via makeup and styling artists who worked with the product. Our aim was to transfer this professionalism and at the same time the manifold facets of feminine beauty into the store."

DESIGN SOLUTION

Angela Kreutz continues:

By using a high contrasting black and white color scheme we emphasized the yin and yang of daily beauty and found, additionally, a very good way to separate the skin care products from the makeup utensils. This makes it easier for the female customers to immediately find what they are looking for. The être belle logo adorns the entry of the store and is also displayed prominently on the back wall. Otherwise, the branding isn't so much about logo placement but is defined through the products and the atmosphere.

The store, which is about 860 sq. ft, is located in the Skyline Plaza in Frankfurt. The design divides the store into two areas, one for makeup and the other for body care products. "This complementary duality is reflected in the design concept starting with the entrance itself: an anthracite gray mat gives contour to the spacious storefront, which rises on one side with a gentle curve only to branch off and turn downward at a sharp right angle. The contrast of opposites carries through to the interior. Starkly geometric walls give way to dynamic curves; dark and light areas alternate just as swiftly; square and round shapes complement one another in charming regularity," says Ms. Kreutz.

The entrance to the makeup area is defined by close-up images with words like "lips," "eyes," and "color," and images of beautiful women are projected against the dark wall. Muted colors of gray, white, and anthracite are complemented by the light oak floors. Delicate furnishings are grouped in altar-like configurations throughout the sales floor, atmospherically decorated with specials and notable products.

More subdued and subtle is the treatment of the body care section of the shop, expressed through delicate, powdery tones, sleekly simple furniture, and refined shelving for the product display. Angela Kreutz explains: "The presentation of the products follows the order in which they are applied. Cleverly, the cabinets follow the course of a conch shell—a semi-circular niche. The body care department remains true to the principle of exciting contrast. The monotone ceiling with strategically aimed spot lighting breaks up a circular depression; the play of light and shadow literally crowns the new store concept. All in all—an exclusive, sensual pleasure." There is also a private area for customer care and spa treatments as well as a relaxation zone situated between the display and checkout area that is harmoniously integrated yet separated by a floor-length, light-colored curtain.

CONCLUSION

For the design firm, it is a "place that equally radiates sophistication and simple elegance. It is the perfect complement to the brand's high quality cosmetic products—with a design that stands for the sheer beauty of every woman. Planning a rollout shop system is about creating a unique look with a high recognition value. By using our principle of soft and edgy lines as well as black and white contrasts the store leaves a long-lasting impression."

Christian Unger, Managing Director of être belle, had this to say about the new store: "We are really totally delighted about the first être belle cosmetics concept store here in Frankfurt. The aim of this concept was to connect an exclusive presentation space with a welcoming 'realm of experience' for women who are interested in cosmetics and especially those who want to become cosmetic fans. In cooperation with the team from Blocher Blocher Shops and View, we even exceeded our expectations. Now, we are looking forward to opening stores in Berlin and Stuttgart and to further expediting our active and sustainable brand building."

DESIGN CREDITS:

Design:	Blocher Blocher Shops, Stuttgart, Germany Angela Kreutz: Head of Communications
Client:	être belle
Visual Merchandising:	Blocher Blocher View, Stuttgart, Germany
Photography:	Joachim Grothus for Blocher Blocher Partners, Stuttgart, Germany

▶ **Figure 1:** Though women have been using the être belle cosmetics and body care products for decades, the brand's first actual retail space recently opened in the Skyline Plaza Mall in Frankfurt, Germany.

▲ **Figure 2:** The light oak wood flooring connects the two areas, with black walls on the left for the makeup and white predominating on the right for body care. The être belle logo, in gold, appears over the cash/wrap counter, and oval and round display tables complement the curved white wall.

▼ **Figure 3:** With the sharp contrast of black and white, the designers emphasized the yin and yang of daily beauty products and used it as a way of separating the makeup from the body care collections. Curved lines contrast with sharp right angles in the rather small space.

▶ **Figure 4:** In the body care area the products are presented in cabinets that follow the course of a conch shell—a semi-circular niche. The monochrome ceiling is outlined with strategically placed spotlights that break up the circular depression. Soft, rounded lines are featured in this area.

▶ **Figure 5:** Body care items are displayed on well-lit shelves and also on the altar-like tables, specials and the newest products being strategically placed to catch customers' attention.

◀ Figure 6: Dramatic black, sharp and edgy lines and large photo blowups plus words like "eyes," "lips," and "color" create the contrasting area for cosmetics. Adding to the "drama" are the decorative attachment lights that illuminate the product display and the theatrical mirror on the table.

◀ Figure 7: The makeup items are clearly displayed and well lit, mirrors allowing customers to try out the products.

▶ Figure 8:
The private area for customer care and spa treatments at the rear of the space is screened from the shop area by a floor-length curtain.

CASE STUDY 1.13

HR2

BROSSARD QUARTIER DIX 30, QUEBEC CITY, CANADA

DESIGN: JANSON GOLDSTEIN LLP, NEW YORK CITY, USA

DESIGN OBJECTIVE

What began almost 180 years ago as a fur shop in Quebec City has evolved into *the* authentic Canadian fashion department store—Holt Renfrew. Today that name or brand is synonymous with luxury, refinement, elegance, and fine merchandise. Recently, Holt Renfrew called upon the NYC-based architectural design firm of Janson Goldstein to come up with an entirely new brand—hr2—a "little sister" to the Holt Renfrew brand—"carrying the DNA but with its own distinct experience and mood," according to Steve Scuro, a partner at Janson Goldstein.

The shop in the Quartier Dix 30 shopping center in Brossard is designed to "reflect the Holt Renfrew's brand 'halo' of luxury and style but engage the customer in a fresh and singular way in order to define hr2 as an entirely new and unique experience," said Mark Janson. He continued:

> *In this case, this is a fully conceived concept that is designed specific to the market: hr2 replaces Holt's previous generation off-price stores—Last Call—with this new concept that is no longer off-price, but rather, conceived to deliver "great brands at value prices." It is meant to feel fashionable, fresh, and distinguishable from other brands. It's a distinctive environment that represents the brand.*

DESIGN SOLUTION

Working with a very cost-effective budget, the designers have come up with an open concept that allows customers to experience the setting all at once (unlike its predecessor). Mark Janson explains: "It's a very fluid space. There is a distinct, overarching architecture and, within that, the merchandise defines each area. It's a holistic approach to the space." The exterior of the store is an articulated "screen" comprised of painted aluminum perforated mesh panels that are folded along the diagonal. These folds create a kinetic play of light and shadow using a very low-tech material. The hr2 company's signature magenta color lights up the façade at night and makes a strong beckoning call to its target market.

Inside, "the store offers a pop art aura against simple white walls and polished concrete," and the 16 ft high ceilings add to the spacious feeling of the store. A winding path initiated by the linear, sculptural ceiling treatment guides shoppers throughout the store's subsections. Steve Scuro adds: "As you walk through, you can glimpse various merchandise throughout the entire store, yet when you are shopping, you're in a space that is more defined and has a more intimate scale." A triangular, sloped wooden "slash" down the center of the space brings the shopper's attention to the unique pop art-inspired graphic wall that encloses the fitting rooms at the rear of the space. At the front of the space and within this ceiling "slash," natural light comes in through clear glass windows set between the exterior and interior perforated panels and fills the selling floor. Janson explains: "After dark, the interior light comingles with the LED uplights on the exterior where the architecture is conceived to create a powerful and unmistakably iconic statement designed to distinguish and support the brand."

Twelve-foot high wood and painted millwork merchandising walls are "floated" below the ceiling and were inspired by a hedged garden maze. Set at assorted angles and alignments to each other, they create "rooms" for special product categories and yet maintain clear sight lines throughout the space. Stretched fabric visuals, fit into frames and highlighted with super-sized graphics, rest above these floating cabinets and synchronized digital "ticker tape" flows through, delivering fashion messages to the shoppers. Throughout there is a mix of youthful and abstract motifs like the bursts of color on the signage and the seemingly animated giant numbers that bounce off the fitting room doors and the pop art mural by UXUS of Amsterdam.

The ceiling-mounted lighting was conceived as a graphic pattern with staggered, "migrating" fluorescent tubes in one dimension, and continuous strut-mounted track lighting in the perpendicular dimension leads patrons from the front to the back of the space. "The pattern-making created by the positioning of the light sources breaks down the scale of the open 24,000 sq. ft ceiling while providing both ambient and focused light conceived to highlight and enhance the merchandise," said Mark Janson.

CONCLUSION

The cumulative effect is a modern, fresh, unique retail environment which engages the customer in many ways and distinguishes a new brand in a crowded and competitive marketplace. Though the store carries more popular priced items than the Holt Renfrew stores, the look and feel of hr2 still reflects the taste level—the refinement and quality—of the mother brand.

DESIGN CREDITS:

Design:	Janson Goldstein LLP, New York City, USA Mark Janson: Partner Steve Scuro: Partner Jason Spangler: Senior Designer
Client:	Holt Renfrew
Executive Architect:	IBI Architects
Pop Art Mural:	UXUS, Amsterdam, The Netherlands
Lighting Designer:	Suzanne Powadluk Design, Inc.
General Contractor:	Pomerleau Inc.
Fixture Contractor:	Luxe Agencement D'Interieur
Photography:	Mikiko Kikuyama

◀ **Figure 1:** The exterior has an articulated screen made up of painted perforated aluminum mesh panels that are illuminated with hr2's signature magenta light at night.

▼ **Figure 2:** A 16 ft high ceiling and an almost all white interior create a sense of spaciousness for the new brand. "It is meant to feel fashionable, fresh and distinguishable from other brands. It's a distinctive environment that represents the brand."

▲ **Figure 3:** A triangular, sloped wooden slash down the center of the space adds to the drama and highlights the staggered pattern of the floating fluorescent light fixtures that lead shoppers to the rear of the space.

◀ **Figure 4:** The 12 ft high painted wood millwork merchandising walls seem to be suspended in space and were inspired by a hedged garden maze.

▲ **Figure 5:** Set at angles and yet aligned to each other, these walls create "rooms" for special category presentations.

◥ **Figure 6:** One of the "rooms" offering product in an intimate scaled area. The brand's concept is no longer "off-price" but "great brands at value prices."

▶ **Figure 7:** In the fitting room area seemingly animated numbers appear to pop off of the individual fitting room doors. The color-filled mural that encloses this space and enhances the store's pop art aura is visible on the right.

CASE STUDY 1.14

BARBISIO FACTORY

CATANIA, ITALY

DESIGN: DUO COMMERCIAL DESIGN, CATANIA, ITALY

DESIGN OBJECTIVE

The Barbisio brand has been around since 1862, starting out as the producer of fine hats and then, a century later, becoming the "go to" place for the finest in men's fashion labels and classic styling. When Barbisio moved into Catania's fashion hub, the opportunity for creating two separate stores catering to two different types of client became a feasible option. The Barbisio Classic store would still carry top Italian and international brands such as Loro Piana, Burberry, and Ballantyne, while the "new concept" store would be the "younger brother" attending to the fashion dictates of a younger and trendier market—both male and female.

Andrea Guardo, a principal in the new design firm DUO Commercial Design who created the new store, explains:

> *Six years after its creation Barbisio New Concept was seeking a more independent and autonomous identity from the "Classic" store and therefore, on approaching the restyling of the interiors, we embraced the challenge of laying the bases of a new brand that would still be related to the original one but, with time, would be growing and developing to affirm itself as an autonomous one.*
>
> *We came up with the idea of reinforcing this aspect—an evolution of the younger brother that is now standing on his own two feet—by also reinforcing the name, and we agreed on "Barbisio Factory" as a way to maintain the original visual cues (logo, graphics, naming) referring to the historical Barbisio but contemporarily declaring a new rising personality that is represented by experimentation, investigation, and research into what is always fresh, new, and distinctive. The new interiors and naming it Barbisio Factory declared such a new "beginning" as a natural and ongoing development from an inherited tradition in style to a more contemporary identity.*

DESIGN SOLUTION

Andrea Guardo continues explaining how the designers created the brand identity for Barbisio Factory: "The concept for the restyling of the interiors of Barbisio Factory was simultaneously generated along with the concept of its brand identity to create a unique product. The client, Antonio Giangreco, felt very comfortable with this approach as he recognized the value of both elements and also the cross-reference between retail interiors and brand identity in terms of future marketing strategies.

"The word 'factory' associated with the name Barbisio calls out for something experimental, something evoking the work of people and a place of production. The store is conceived as a place for producing styles for different customers who aren't afraid to 'build' or reinforce their own look by combining both bespoke and new labels. 'Factory' also refers to a place where the idea of transformation is the core principle: a transformation of the original historical brand (Barbisio) into a new one that is an elaboration of the former; transformation of a spatial experience with a new interior that incorporates different existing and newly specifically designed elements; transformation of the store imagined as a showcase, an erratic warehouse where vintage furniture and contemporary displays provide a stimulating environment for a personalized shopping experience.

"Mostly importantly, all these influential cues have been combined to create a different spatial experience within the shop. There are two main new features in the store that are conceived as a unique system creating a pattern for the customer's journey and browsing into the store. We have imagined a central display as a kind of catwalk that develops around a structural column. The geometry and silhouettes are intended to resemble the combination of mechanical components, twisting around the column and thus emphasizing the perspective from the entrance toward the back of the store. This element is useful for the display of different articles and it acts as a sort of stage for different uses including live performances. Further to this new display area (which was one of the critical requests in the client's brief), we have also incorporated a workstation in this central position that acts both as a welcoming desk and a cash counter.

"The window display areas are also conceived as part of this new system both in terms of shape and material. They are imagined as continuous podiums projecting through the windows and also redefine the appearance of the external façade with the new signage.

"All new elements have wood structures and surfaces and they result from a combination of two finishes: the bases are rendered with a product much like 'stucco veneziano' paint, in a light concrete-gray tone and finished with a protective film of decorative wax. The upper part of the main display and other moveable parts incorporated in the window showcases are white lacquered. Along the perimeter of the store the hanging device systems are designed and created with steel rods with a transparent varnish, whereas existing shelves are in painted natural wood. The preferred color palette of new elements merges perfectly with the existing laminate flooring and wooden furniture; the bright white walls and ceiling create a counterpoint to the intense tones of the floor. A newly improved lighting scheme adds value to both the merchandise and the cozy atmosphere of the store."

CONCLUSION

Guardo says: "Barbisio Factory is the result of the development of the existing brand and is a perfect example showing a 'new direction' for expanding the market in terms of customers and in terms of products on offer. The existing customer base is also retained because of the continuity of the quality of the products and the quality of the service. The identification of Barbisio in the 'new brand' is thus a symbol of continuity of a tradition in style and service."

DESIGN CREDITS:

Design:	DUO Commercial Design, Catania, Italy Andrea Guardo: Project Designer Giuseppe Brischetto: Assistant Designer
Client:	Antonio Giangreco at Barbisio Factory
Photography:	Salvatore Gozzo

◀ **Figure 1:** In looking to define a new brand with an established brand as part of its name, Barbisio Factory presents a new look for young, trendy shoppers in Catania.

◀ **Figure 2:** "'Factory' suggests something experimental—something evoking the work of people—a place of production." The store was conceived as a place where customers can build their outfits in their own style.

▲ **Figure 3:** The fixtures act as places of display but also transform the spatial experience in the shop, while the catwalk built around the supporting column serves as the fulcrum of the design. Part of the central space was designed to serve as a welcoming desk and a cash counter. The squared hanging devices, attached to the perimeter walls, are made of stainless steel rods. The new lighting scheme not only accentuates the merchandise but adds a "cozy atmosphere" to the store.

◀ **Figure 4:** The white walls and ceiling are complemented by the natural wood shelves and the concrete gray finish of the bases and the deeper gray of the existing laminate flooring.

▶ **Figure 5:** This new interior also combines the use of different existing and newly designed pieces creating "an erratic warehouse where vintage furniture and contemporary designed displays provide a stimulating environment for a personalized shopping experience."

PART 2

A Brand Makeover

CASE STUDIES

The brand has been around for some time ... then someone in the company realizes that the brand has become tired, stale, and passé. Maybe it has kept its traditional clientele—but like the brand, the customers are showing their age. Younger, new, and more with-it shoppers are walking by and not stopping. When they know the brand name but associate it with their parents and "old," it is time for a makeover: a rejuvenation—a freshening up. But a brand that has been around for a while and has built a solid reputation does not want to lose the faithful clients it has garnered over the years in its search for a newer, younger, trendier, and expanding market. What to do?

Aéropostale is far from being a dowdy, tired brand, but the design team at GH+A was challenged to reinvent the brand image as being more fashion conscious while never losing sight of the basics on which the brand has built its solid reputation. The new store had to appear as though created for the local customer and not feel like part of an impersonal corporation. The design team used materials that suggested an earlier time and complemented them with old signs and timber from a long-gone seaside boardwalk. Though the appeal was to Long Island shoppers, there were constant reminders of New York City and its exciting appeal.

It was in the hope of building a "stronger connection with its creative 'imaginista' customers" and emphasizing the brand's playful personality that **House of Kipling** employed the UXUS design firm to design their new retail store. With the mischievous monkey logo scampering throughout the space and mundane objects used in surprising ways, and with frames used to highlight new products, the net result is a bright, fun setting that is sure to satisfy a new audience and amuse an established client.

In its search for a new brand identity, **Monton** wanted a concept that would highlight the brand's new attributes. It fell to the design firm dan pearlman Markenarchitektur to come up with a design that would suggest "inspiring, cosmopolitan, and seductive" to the desired target market. With the theme of "Cosmopolitan Jetsetters" and the new flag logo and a bright and colorful interior, Monton was on its way to being a brand that was "at home in the world."

Buffalo Wild Wings wanted "to update its identity and restaurant environment to support its positioning as the ultimate social experience for sports fans" and make it a more "friendly" place. By adding elements like carpeting in the dining areas, letting in the daylight, and other subtle touches, the setting became more accessible for lunches, yet with the constant bombardment of sports activities on the numerous flat-screen TVs— and BWW maintained its sporting image.

Solara's previous stores were "flavorless and bland." Opting to appear in a mall where many noted brands appeared at their best, Solara needed "distinction" and a more upscale look. The concern was that the "new and stylish and upgraded look of the shop would defeat a very important aspect of the brand—value pricing." The challenge was how to look better for a new market but still maintain the value and price inherent in the brand. A more sophisticated setting, smart neutral palette, an eye-catching ceiling, and the new tagline—"Sois éblouissante!" (Be dazzling!)—seem to work, along with the wide-open façade.

It was all about creating a brand identity that truly represented the location the brand inhabited. Thus, the concept was to turn the rather unexciting dining space at the **Barbican** into a dining destination befitting the location. The designers at SHH Architects, working closely with garden designer Kate Gould, turned the bi-level space into two distinctly different restaurants with outdoor patios that tie it all together. The ground level cafe is now the informal, dine-in or takeaway Barbican Foodhall and the upper level is the more elegant Barbican Lounge. Together they "bring the Centre's food and beverage offer up to the level of the Barbican's long-established worldwide reputation for art exhibitions and performances."

It was a matter of preserving history in re-energizing the **Oakville Grocery** while making sure "to retain all the unique character—and still remember it as it was." Tradition and heritage and ties to the past can and will work for some brands, while for others it is better left in the past. The Oakville Grocery is steeped in history and though it has been contemporized to make it work more efficiently and safely, it still retains much of its past—now not-so-faded—charm. Similarly,

Sandbar needed to be updated for the twenty-first century while retaining its historic charm. Here, the designers brought touches of the past into a relatively fresh and rehabilitated space.

DORMA, with its century and more years of leadership in its industry, felt the need to update—to leave the past in the past and look forward to the future with its new brand identity and new credo: "From Today to Tomorrow." There is nothing old-fashioned about the slick, contemporary trade show stand created for them.

The challenge that faced the designers at Burdifilek was how to "elevate and rejuvenate **Bell**'s branded retail environment" and reflect "the approachable, clean lines of the brand's new corporate identity." With the use of the strong yet limited color palette featuring Bell's signature blue color and clean, sharp lines, the designers created the new striking setting for Bell products and services.

Domino's gave up the "pizza" in its name but retained the domino logo and its color palette. "Domino's wanted to communicate real change with its store environment" and to show that Domino's is part of their diners' lives and part of the community. With its community wall and local touches, it now is the "local" pizzeria—a definite part of the neighborhood and a member of the community.

Sometimes it is a matter of getting a new and fresh look. It can be as little as a few subtle changes but with enough of the original concept still recognizable and familiar—like the Domino's logo with "Pizza" erased. Then again, it can be more a matter of retaining the brand's heritage and emphasizing its history, as was done in Sandbar. Monton and Solara represent totally new looks for brand identities that no longer do what they used to do. But, whatever the reason, the balance has to be maintained between keeping the customers you have and attracting new ones.

CASE STUDY 2.1

AÉROPOSTALE

ROOSEVELT FIELD, LONG ISLAND, NEW YORK, USA

DESIGN: GH+A DESIGN, MONTREAL, CANADA

DESIGN OBJECTIVE

Aéropostale, a mall-based retailer of casual apparel targeted at teenagers, opened another store recently in the Roosevelt Field Shopping Center on Long Island, just east of New York City. With almost 1000 stores covering the United States, Canada, and Puerto Rico—plus more spreading out in Europe, the Middle East, and Asia—the company maintains its proprietary brands by designing, sourcing, marketing, and selling its own merchandise.

For the new store, GH+A Design of Montreal was challenged to design a new prototype that would help reinvent Aéropostale's image "as being more fashion conscious while never losing sight of the basics for which the brand has built its solid reputation." Debbie Kalisky, Director of Retail Development at GH+A, explains: "The objective was to have the store appear as though it had been created for the local customer and not feel like part of an impersonal corporation. The store 'speaks' to the local teenager by creating a community experience that goes beyond merchandise."

DESIGN SOLUTION

Jonathan Knodell, Senior Designer on this project, explains: "Aéropostale is for everyone. As a brand it is open, accessible, and inviting. Aéropostale has embraced fashion and has incorporated more trend-right—even trend-forward—styles into its merchandise mix alongside its beloved branded basics. As always, the brand offers the same compelling value which Aero customers have come to expect." When asked, "How well does the design deliver on the brand promise?" Knodell answered:

> *The Aéropostale brand is seamlessly integrated in the store design. Inlaid penny tile at the entrance floor evokes a sense of New York City heritage. Custom A87 graphics on the steamer trunk provides subtle brand reinforcement. Details in the line drawings on the fitting room wall coverings pay homage to Aéropostale's NYC heritage, as do brand icons such as their adored bulldog mascot. Weathered graphic panels on the sides of*

fixtures allude to the fixture's "previous life." Individual fixtures are covertly branded and blend into the overall design. Rather than newly applied graphics, the intent was to have the messaging appear worn as if they had already been there for years—reinforcing a sense of authenticity and minimalizing the feeling of a corporate/chain store image.

The store has been divided into five distinct zones or rooms. Stepping off the mall aisle, the shopper steps into the Entry Room, which is actually a wide display area filled with headless mannequins—both male and female—sporting the newest collections. There are also the community boards with relevant topics regarding local talent, community "heroes," charities looking for volunteers, and local news items. The brand's newest collections are presented in the next room, the Fashion Room. Maintaining a high density of product is important to reinforce the value aspect of the brand, and thus the flexible fixtures have multiple tiers and nesting elements. The catwalk or runway feature table is constructed from reclaimed wood from the iconic New York symbol—the boardwalk at Coney Island. The Swing Room has the temporary feeling of a pop-up shop, which adds a sense of excitement. It is here that the denim and seasonal collections are on view under a swag of electric wires festooned with bare bulbs. The Heritage Room focuses on Aéropostale's core, logo-driven product line, while the Live, Love, Dream Room for girls "is a whole experience unto itself with custom line art illustrations of typical cast iron, SoHo columns." Ms. Kalisky adds, "The furniture provides bright pops of color coordinated with the bold merchandise in this room. Inside the fitting rooms, meticulously detailed line art murals depict apartments from various neighborhoods around New York City." These line-drawn environments suggest an artist's apartment in the West Village, the pad of a Park Slope photographer, the home of a wannabe Carrie Bradshaw in SoHo, the factory loft of a Williamsburg hipster musician and a budding actress from East Village. In the fitting rooms, iPads allow each shopper to choose his or her own music so that each fitting room becomes a private listening booth as well.

CONCLUSION

The store design connects with the teenage shopper both in a fashion sense and in a socially relevant manner. Debbie Kalisky comments: "It creates a community experience that goes beyond merchandise and also connects with its customer by offering them the opportunity to make a personal contribution to the overall customer experience by voting for their favorite songs on iPads to be featured on the playlist while shopping the store. A dynamic and unconventional storefront design was a key factor in capturing the imagination of mall shoppers and it instantly conveys the message that

Aéropostale has turned the page and has moved in an exciting new direction."

ICSC (International Council of Shopping Centers), in awarding this Aéropostale design its Silver award in the Retail Store Design category, stated that the

> *store concept has revamped the brand's image, creating an emotional connection with their target market. The dual notions of community and in-store technology have redefined the shopping experience through old-school style board posting, and new-school iPads, allowing shoppers to select personal style playlists while they shop in the store, watch Aero videos, browse suggested outfit ensembles, and read reviews. There are also two iMac computers in the sales area where shoppers can visit pre-selected websites to volunteer for charity work, visit the e-commerce site and view online exclusive offers.*

DESIGN CREDITS:

Design:	GH+A Design Steve Sutton: Partner Jonathan Knodell: Senior Designer France Delorme: Director of Resources Matthieu Berthelot and Genevieve Trudeau-Drolet: Designers Debbie Kalisky: Director of Retail Development
Client:	Aéropostale Tom Johnson: CEO Mary Jo Pile: Executive VP, Customer Engagement Emelia Fabricant: Executive VP, Brand Mark Dorwart: Senior VP Logistics, Real Estate, and Construction Tim Anderson: VP Store Development Jeff Lee: VP Visual Merchandising Scott Birnbaum: Senior VP Marketing Robert Ruscher: Director of Construction
Architect:	Lami Grubb Architects, Pittsburgh, Pennsylvania, USA
General Contractor:	Terry Adams Inc., Elizabethtown, Kentucky, USA
Custom Wall Covering:	PCL Graphics, Chicago and Coloredge, New York City, USA
Artwork Wallpaper Fitting Rooms:	Edward Kulczycki, Mind's Eye Studio, Canton, Michigan, USA
Photography:	Déjà Vu Studios, Mineola, New York, USA

◀ **Figure 1:** The inlaid white penny tile floor at the entrance and the reclaimed brick walls evoke a sense of the brand's heritage. Also, the old-fashioned, pressed-tin ceilings suggest something old for the very new.

▼ **Figure 2:** "Open, accessible, and inviting" is the new Aéropostale shop, with a look through to the various zones inside. Note the community boards with relevant local heroes, topics, and events dominating the left wall.

◀ **Figure 3:** Weathered graphic panels on the sides of fixtures allude to the signs' previous use, and the illuminated "windows" over the wall-hung garments further the "loft look."

▶ **Figure 4:** The Girl's Room is a fun and special place filled with decorative line drawings, bright color, and unusual touches. The cast iron columns of SoHo are evident throughout.

▲ Figure 5: A shocking-pink Statue of Liberty and the theme "Live, Love, Dream" scrawled on the ceiling add to the unique quality of the space.

◀ Figure 6: Detailed line-drawn murals suggesting apartments of various types of women living in different areas of New York line the walls of the fitting rooms, which are also equipped with iPads so that shoppers can select their own music.

CASE STUDY 2.2

BUFFALO WILD WINGS

CINCINNATI, OHIO, USA

DESIGN: FITCH, COLUMBUS, OHIO, USA

DESIGN OBJECTIVE

Buffalo Wild Wings, a Minneapolis-based sports-type bar and restaurant that has been around for over 30 years, wanted "to update its identity and restaurant environment to support its positioning as the ultimate social experience for sports fans." Part of that challenge was creating a sports-centric space that was also more customer friendly. The appeal had to go beyond the usual bar crowd. To accomplish this, they called upon FITCH of Columbus, Ohio, an architectural design firm.

DESIGN SOLUTION

When asked what FITCH does for a client with regard to the client's brand, Christian Davies, Executive Creative Director for the Americas for FITCH said: "Our work on brand development runs the gamut from birthing new brands, to polishing, redirecting, and reinventing new ones. We take the values and goals of that company and unite them in a cohesive visual language." The new identity meant a new environment and new graphics; and the familiar buffalo coin that served as a logo got a makeover. "The buffalo itself was also beefed up and has a little more 'tude."

In creating the new look for Buffalo Wild Wings (BWW), Christian Davies explains:

> *It may sound simplistic, but any design should always be aligned with the customer. If the goal of evolving the brand is to retain that customer then the work should continue to be rooted in their needs and desires. If the goal is to evolve to reach a new customer, with different needs, the reinvention would need to reflect that.*

There are carpeted areas at the sides for relaxed dining while the central bar area has hard flooring for a more energetic experience. Also, the windows and natural lighting make the restaurant seem less bar-like and makes the place more comfortable at lunchtime.

The new design—the Stadia concept—was inspired by the stadium experience and it starts with the "tunnel" entrance that is scaled and proportioned like a team entry into a stadium. "Guests hear the energy of the restaurant and glimpse activity while they wait." Adding to the imagery are the locker room benches provided for seating. The materials, colors, and environmental graphics all support the stadium experience. "It's high contrast, large scale, bold, immersive and iconic." Or, as Davies says: "The goal is rarely to literally interpret the brand through the elements of the design. The best experiences embody a brand's essence in more subtle ways—reflecting its tone, values, and personality through the combination of elements that bring the environment to life"—like the stadium for sports fans who can tap into the energy and social experience of sports events with easy access to beer and wings in the comparative comfort of the bar/restaurant. Davies adds: "In today's market any and all the consumer's senses can and should be activated. We are seeing customers embracing brands that provide 'real' physical experiences, and touching the senses is an incredibly powerful way to do that."

Adding to the brand's sporting experience, and as audible and visual sensory cues, are the banks of large screens and the enhanced AV system throughout the restaurant, the jumbo screen at the bar, and the local high school and university team memorabilia near the tunnel entrance. Other attractions that play up the taste and smell senses are the BWW signature sauces and draught beer. The sauces are displayed in a showcase at the tunnel entrance and the beer wall in the bar area.

CONCLUSION

The new concept "captures the essence and energy of the game. With sports as the focal point, the environment creates a social and local gathering place for true fans and makes the BWW experience unique." It sums up the BWW tagline, "Wings. Beer. Sports."

DESIGN CREDITS:

Design: FITCH, Columbus, Ohio, USA
Christian Davies: Executive Creative Director for the Americas
Stephen Jay: Managing Director
Ryan Brazelton: Design Director
David Vilkama: Design Director
Brian Connell: Senior Designer
Luis Enfante / Erin Wilson / Carly Tysh: Designers
Romano Klepec: Project Manager
Client: Buffalo Wild Wings
Architect: FITCH, Phoenix, Arizona, USA
Lighting Design: Lighting Design Alliance, Long Beach, California, USA
Lighting: FD Lawrence Electric, Cincinnati, Ohio, USA; and Hill Phoenix, Covington, Georgia, USA
Graphics: Eclipse Corp., Gahanna, Ohio, USA
Memorabilia: Collection Connection Frame Shop, Oregon City, USA
Photography: Mark Steele Photography, Columbus, Ohio, USA

◀ **Figure 1:** The brief for the new look for Buffalo Wild Wings was to create a sports-centric place that would be more friendly and have an appeal beyond the bar crowd. Take-out has its own easily located logo yellow window.

▲ **Figure 3:** There are zoned dining spaces with hard flooring around the energetic bar and carpeted floors for the relaxed dining areas. Windows in the latter areas allow in natural light and make the space seem less bar-like and more acceptable to the lunchtime crowd.

◀ **Figure 2:** The entry is designed like the tunnel entrance into a stadium. Guests can hear the energy coming out of the restaurant as well as glimpse the excitement of the diners and the action pictured on many TV screens. The locker room bench provides seating for waiting guests.

▲ **Figure 4:** There are banks of large TV screens and an enhanced AV system to satisfy the sports-oriented guests. On the far right is the desk where guests check in. The bar is at the rear.

▶ **Figure 5:** A view of the relaxed seating area and the printed table top with the brand's "birth" date. The look and feel of the new brand identity is designed to stand beside national sports teams and sporting products.

▶ **Figure 6:** The bar is centrally located and the heart of the space. Jumbo screens fill the space above the bar. With sports as the focal point, BWW is a social and local gathering place and makes the brand's tagline ring clear; "Wings. Beer. Sports."

CASE STUDY 2.3

HOUSE OF KIPLING

29 BROMPTON ROAD, LONDON, UK

DESIGN: UXUS, AMSTERDAM, THE NETHERLANDS

DESIGN OBJECTIVE

The House of Kipling started in Antwerp, Belgium back in 1987 and picked the name Kipling for their luggage line because it was easy to pronounce in any language and because Rudyard Kipling's *Jungle Book* was popular. The monkey with the curled tail became its logo and talisman. The company felt it was time to create a new home for the Kipling brand that "reinforces the brand's playful personality and builds a stronger connection with its creative 'imaginista' customers."

DESIGN SOLUTION

A visit to the new retail concept on Brompton Road in London takes the Kipling world-famous luggage brand to a different place and time. "We wanted to express the values of the Kipling consumer in a retail experience they would be inspired to shop in. The House of Kipling is a domestic approach to retail, encouraging discovery and exploration in-store." The new design concept was created by the Amsterdam-based UXUS design firm, and George Gottl, Chief Creative Officer of UXUS, continues:

> *Our solution was to create a new home for the Kipling brand. We reinterpreted best retail practices into a domestic approach—using vernacular of a home for fixtures and product displays. The new concept takes a fresh perspective on everyday things and mundane and familiar objects are put in surprising contexts that create an unexpected visual story and showcase the product range.*

The product presentation is displayed as "Kipling Family Portraits"—and new arrivals are presented in their own new frames. A kitchen table serves as the cash/wrap desk and travel items are stacked on a quirky luggage trolley. The dressing area suggests a cozy living room with colorful poufs, full-length mirrors, and a large, warm rug. "Individual touches like chests of drawers, coat stands, and candy jars with monkey souvenirs encourage customer interaction and discovery." The "Whimsy Wall" is a pin-up board where shoppers can share their thoughts and pleasures with all things Kipling.

The new visual identity and Kipling packaging was inspired by the Kipling monkey, the iconic brand element. According to George Gottl,

> *The signature brand pattern features uniform rows of monkeys in a neutral color palette with an occasional color-pop fun monkey. The pattern appears on the façade and in-store on furniture, fixtures, and even as table legs on the check-out counter. Additionally, the pattern is applied to packaging, labels, product backdrops, and digital/print material. The signature serif typography, used for in-store call-outs, is reminiscent of the Kipling monkey's tail. Occasionally, on highlighted words, a silhouette of the monkey interacts with the word. The branded color palette is used to represent the two sides of the Kipling brand. White, cool, and neutral colors represent Kipling's sophisticated side, while bright Pantone colors express the "fun" aspect of the brand.*

The heritage of the brand is emphasized by the materials selected for the new retail space. There are the Flemish-inspired wall tiles, varnished oak, ceramic tiles, and rugs that "create a homey feel," as well as the bright colors that "inject joy and playfulness to the space." Gottl sums it up thus: "The House of Kipling celebrates everyday creativity and invites visitors to use their imagination in a new way. The retail experience embraces the cheerfulness of Kipling customers and encourages them to play with their personal style."

CONCLUSION

With a rollout of this concept already planned, Kipling executive, Richard Macey, had this to say about the new retail brand identity: "UXUS has a real creative vision which perfectly matched the objective of the Kipling team to produce a concept which told the rich Kipling story to our global consumers, while being cost effective in production, easy to replicate globally, and adaptable to many store and shop-in-shop executions with varying levels of stock density."

DESIGN CREDITS:

Design:	UXUS, Amsterdam, The Netherlands George Gottl: Chief Creative Officer Oliver Michell: Chief Creative Officer/Architect
Client:	House of Kipling Richard Macey: VP/General Manager
Photography:	Dim Balsem

◀ **Figure 1:** There are monkeys a-plenty roaming in and around the new House of Kipling store. On the shop's façade they appear in rows of neutral colors with an occasional one popping out in full color.

◀ **Figure 2:** Using a "domestic approach" to the retail design, everyday objects are used in unexpected ways to create a unique visual story. Drawers, chests, kitchen tables, coat stands, and other mundane objects serve as fixtures.

◀ **Figure 3:** White walls and floors are highlighted by fresh, bright pastel colors. Featured products are emphasized by oval frames that step out from the wall displays.

◀ **Figure 4:**

Drawers serve as platforms, collectors, or presenters and add to the homey feeling that the designers underlined as being important.

◀ **Figure 5:** The monkey logo appears on poufs, as cut-outs, or printed on packaging material. Here in the sitting area oval metal frames, poufs, and mirrors plus shots of pastel colors make the area a delightful spot.

▶ **Figure 6:** A kitchen table, painted white, plus a chest of drawers serves as the cash/wrap desk. A freestanding white logo monkey steps out on its own. The Whimsy Wall appears behind the counter.

CASE STUDY 2.4

DOMINO'S

HOUSTON, TEXAS, USA

DESIGN: CHUTE GERDEMAN, COLUMBUS, OHIO, USA

DESIGN OBJECTIVE

A few years ago, Domino Pizza, though a well known and highly advertised name brand, wasn't doing so well in the market. The brand was mainly recognized as a "take-out/delivery" operation rather than a "sit-down/dine-in" restaurant experience, and thus the Domino Pizza stores were rather cold and uninviting. Pizza eaters couldn't watch the pizza-making process and visually connect with their food. A change was necessary in the store design to create a better brand identity for the revitalized Domino's (without the Pizza) brand.

DESIGN SOLUTION

Lynn Rosenbaum, VP of Environments at the Chute Gerdeman design organization, explains: "We wanted to reflect the goodness of Domino's pizza within the space. In order to do that we had to show how the pizzas were made. The local pizzerias were getting all the credit for natural ingredients. Domino's had all that, but no one knew because of the way its pizzas were presented." He goes on:

> *By the time they came to us they knew a lot about what was working and what wasn't. With an expanded menu, an entirely new recipe for its pizza, and an increased emphasis on using technology and social media to interact with its customers, Domino's wanted to communicate real change with a new store environment to show how they believe in "over-delivering on fresh." The current front counter—serving more as a barricade than a useful surface—and kitchen—hidden behind a wall of pizza boxes—wasn't creating the conducive environment that was needed for this to be accomplished.*

What was missing here was "the sensory experience of pizza making."

Turning the counter 90 degrees opened up the store to customers and "now, the customers can place their order at the newly designed service counter and watch Domino's pizza chefs make their orders." Rosenbaum adds, "By bringing the kitchen front and center and creating a Pizza Theater, we let guests see the best thing Domino's does—making pizza. We allow the customer to go back into the kitchen—literally—and watch the process of pressing the dough, applying the ingredients and putting the pizza in the oven. The customer becomes part of his or her pizza and feels good knowing exactly what went into it. It's a feast for the senses that Domino's never got credit for." The Domino's signature red awning marks off the Pizza Theater with white letters saying "Order" or "Pick Up," and linear pendant light unit, in stainless steel, runs the length of the case directly under the awning, highlighting the area and making it "a glowing beacon" in the otherwise dimly lit store. Under more bright lights, more stainless steel ovens and work stations are played up in the kitchen.

The by now familiar logo—the tilted domino tile, part red and part blue with white dots—today is usually shown without the "Domino's Pizza" block beneath it, and only the Domino's name beneath the tile in blue. Russell Weiner, Domino's Chief Marketing Officer, explains: "So much of our menu is beyond pizza right now that we feel we're more than just a pizza place." Domino's original red, white, and blue color palette has now been warmed up with a "fresh-baked ocher color that the design team calls 'crust'." According to Lynn Rosenbaum, the use of white subway tiles in the kitchen area signifies "fresh and clean," while the red and ocher "create a warm and welcoming atmosphere." This new addition—"crust"—to the Domino's color palette highlights the brand wall, where typography and illustration call out menu items and entertaining pizza facts for customers. A chalkboard wall offers a creative outlet for kids of all ages and features a regularly updated "Pizza Proverb," while Domino's heritage photography is framed nearby. The wall-mounted faux pizza pans that carry phrases and questions ("What's for dessert?") sit level with the dining bar, which is located across from the Pizza Theater. Depending upon the size of the store, some stores will have the dining bar while others will have tables and chairs set out in the red and black dining area. Open refrigerated display cases highlight Domino's new grab-and-go items.

CONCLUSION

Rosenbaum says: "Because the design makes it easy for employees to engage with customers, Domino's feels like a local player in any neighborhood—anywhere. A local tone of voice used in the brand communications helps establish a neighborhood language inside the store and helps to eliminate the feel of a big chain." So, no matter where the basic new store concept gets rolled out, it quickly becomes a neighborhood "local" and the Domino's new brand is quickly familiar and at home. "We want customers to feel like Domino's is more a part of their lives; that they want to go there—it's fun. If we can create the idea that people want Domino's to be part of their lives, then we've accomplished what we set out to do. Customers who were surveyed scored the new Domino's high in both improved brand perception and their likelihood to recommend Domino's to others."

DESIGN CREDITS:

Design:	Chute Gerdeman, Columbus, Ohio, USA
	Wendy Johnson: EVP Account Management and COO
	Lynn Rosenbaum: VP, Environments
	Mindi Trank: VP, Brand and Consumer Strategy
	Steve Pottschmidt: VP, Design Development
	David Birnbaum: Director of Architecture
	Corey Dehus: Creative Director, Brand Communications
	Katie Clements: Senior Designer, Materials Specialist
	Steve Johnson: Senior Designer, Design Implementation
	Renee Kinkopf: Designer, Brand Communications
Client:	Domino's
	Russell Weiner: Chief Marketing Officer
	Brandon Solano: VP, Marketing and Innovation
	Scott Hinshaw: EVP, Franchise Development
	Amber Gadsby: Director of Marketing
	Tim Krause: Director of Store Construction
	Gus Kandah: Manager Capital Sales and Purchasing
	Amber McDonald: Corporate Real Estate Manager
	Alan Okon: Midwest Area Leader, Store Development
	Stephanie Raupp: Retail Marketing Specialist
Architect:	CG Architecture, Columbus, Ohio, USA
	Michael McCall
Photography:	Mark Steele at Mark A. Steele Photography, Columbus, Ohio, USA

◀ **Figure 1:**
The "Pizza" is gone from the sign but the signature red color and the domino logo are still evident in the new look for the familiar brand. Changes in the store design were needed to create a better brand identity for the revitalized brand.

◀ **Figure 2:**
By turning the counter 90 degrees, the store feels more open. Now it is possible to watch the pizzas being made under the illuminated signature red canopy that is "a glowing beacon."

▶ **Figure 3:**
Added to the familiar Domino palette is the warm "crust" color. The white subway tiles in the kitchen area signify "fresh and clean" while the red and ocher colors "create a warm and welcoming" atmosphere. Pizza pans with menu items decorate the "crust" wall.

▶ **Figure 4:**
The chalkboard wall, located opposite the pick-up counter, offers patrons a place to express themselves while waiting. Framed images of Domino's heritage add to the brand's identity as well as offering interest and color.

▲ **Figure 5:** Looking toward the front of the store. The red and black dining area up front varies with the amount of space in the store. The new brand look is friendly yet still familiar and designed to be "a neighborhood local."

CASE STUDY 2.5

BELL

TORONTO, CANADA

DESIGN: BURDIFILEK, TORONTO, CANADA

DESIGN OBJECTIVE

"Because our bricks-and-mortar locations are permanent billboards for our brand, we wanted a store that lived up to our goal to be recognized by customers as Canada's leading telecommunications company," says Devorah Lithwick, VP of Marketing Communications for Bell. When Bell felt the need to "elevate and rejuvenate" the company's branded retail environment, they called upon the creative services of Burdifilek of Toronto. This top Canadian retail design firm accepted the challenge "to create a store design that reflects the approachable, clear lines of the brand's new corporate identity and showcase Bell's products and services."

DESIGN SOLUTION

In order to "stand out in the marketplace and be instantly recognizable," the Burdifilek design team started with a simple color palette of blue, white, gray, and black, signature materials and "an expressively form-driven vocabulary to create an environment that is uniquely Bell." The look and feel of "the overall environment is warm and approachable." The signature Bell blue attracts people on the street where a transparent blue-tinted Starfire glass screen serves as a backdrop for the window displays. From outside it is also possible to see the over-sized, back-lit Bell logo that runs the length of the store and "provides an instant connection back to the brand." Inside the store, explains Diego Burdi, Creative Partner at Burdifilek: "We developed easy-to-navigate, intuitive product displays and touch-screen messaging to ensure easy access to product information. The mid-floor fixturing also encourages a sense of discovery as shoppers move from one zone to the next." Referencing the ergonomics of an actual mobile device, the visual vocabulary of the fixtures mimics the product itself. The typically black and silver products seem to pop out off of the white Corian-topped counters. Though these counters allow shoppers to be served in the traditional manner, it is also easy to "service the customer shoulder to shoulder or face to face, encouraging more friendly personalized contact." The display surfaces are kept uncluttered and allow shoppers free access and interaction with the live products on view. The displays help compartmentalize the product offering while providing flexibility in introducing new technologies as they evolve. Behind the cash desk, suggesting "the personality and warmth of the brand message," is a collage of floating white cubes enhanced with the smiling faces usually seen on Bell product packaging. "The sculptural quality of the interior fittings establishes a point of memory in the minds of customers."

CONCLUSION

Burdifilek's Managing Partner, Paul Filek, says:

> *We have created an authoritative statement for the brand that has a definite "wow factor." The connection back to Bell's corporate identity was top priority; current and future advertising campaigns will be showcased within this design as they become part of the overall architecture. The real success of this concept is in the details and in the overwhelmingly positive reactions from our client and Bell's customers alike.*

Speaking for Bell, Devorah Lithwick adds: "Burdifilek responded with a design that builds on our brand platform, using dozens of subtle elements—like modular fixtures, dramatic lighting, innovative materials, and photos of faces from our packaging. In this way the store looks and feels aligned with—and reinforces—our brand, plus it gives the space the warm, human feeling that is at the heart of our business."

DESIGN CREDITS:

Design:	Burdifilek, Toronto, Ontario, Canada
	Diego Burdi: Creative Partner
	Paul Filek: Managing Partner
	Tom Yip: Senior Designer
	Anthony Tey, Anna Nomerovsky, and Daniel Mei: CADD
	Jacky Kwong: Junior Designer
Client:	Bell
	Devorah Lithwick, VP, Marketing Communication
Photography:	Ben Rahn at A-Frame Studio

◀ **Figure 1:** To "stand out and be instantly recognizable," the new Bell brand corporate identity is dramatically presented in the store in blue, white, gray, and black. The signature blue serves as a come-on to shoppers on the street.

◀ **Figure 2:** The designers used "an expressively form-driven vocabulary to create an environment that is uniquely Bell." Shoppers are encouraged to interact with the various Bell products.

▶ **Figure 3:** The designers developed "easy-to-navigate, intuitive product displays and touch-screen messaging to ensure easy access to product information."

▶ **Figure 4:** The white Corian-topped fixtures and counters make an effective contrast with the traditionally black and silver products on display. The counters also make it possible to serve shoppers "shoulder to shoulder."

◀ **Figure 5:** The cash/wrap desk backed with photos of faces that appear in the brand's ads. Past and present advertising campaigns are showcased in the space and the graphics become part of the architecture.

◀ **Figure 6:** The illuminated Bell wall. It is the dramatic contrast between the letters and the Bell blue wall behind it that serve as a brand reminder for shoppers coming in or going out.

CASE STUDY 2.6

MONTON

ST. PETERSBURG, RUSSIA

DESIGN: DAN PEARLMAN MARKENARCHITEKTUR, BERLIN, GERMANY

DESIGN OBJECTIVE

"Upgrading Monton's visual identity and creating the new store concept is very important for brand development and strengthening its export capability." That was said by Maire Milder, Branding and Retail Developing Director and member of the managing board of the Baltika Group. This fashion developer and retailer is well known throughout Eastern and Central Europe, and especially in the Balkans and Russia, by several brand names including Mosaic, Baltman, Bastion, and Monton. To be able to attract the desired young market in the expanding area, Monton needed a fresh, new look and the brand needed an overhaul as well. Milder adds, "We are updating all Monton existing stores based on the new branding and store concept elements."

DESIGN SOLUTION

Speaking for the design team of the dan pearlman Markenarchitektur of Berlin, Volker Katschinski, Creative Director (Retail) and Founder/Associate of this design firm who worked on the St. Petersburg store, says: "It was essential to analyze the attributes and characteristics of the brand carefully and understand it in depth before it was possible to create a new brand identity." The start for the creation of this brand's new identity, which attracts both fashionable young men and women, was marked by creating new brand attributes—inspiring, cosmopolitan, and seductive. "These formed the basis for a completely new brand and its specific features for the store design and visual communication." "Cosmopolitan Jetsetters" was then created as the brand motto and, as Katschinski explains, "It is used to describe Monton as a brand that is at home in the world, made up of people that are inhabitants of the fictional Monton country and, thus, members of a community of mind; in coherence with that, an overall idea needed to be developed in order to cater to the needs and wants of the Monton target group." Going along with the backstory of this fictional Monton country, a new logo was developed out of a flag made up of double stripes. Depending upon collection and image, a different set of flags is used and the basic flag design was adapted into a general labeling concept for the brand. As Volker Katschinski explains: "The stripes are key elements to the brand appearance and its distinctive look. Rotated by 30 degrees, green and crisp yellow together with gray form the primary colors of the new Monton. Specific color accents always relate to a distinct collection with a seasonal, bright color keyed to the primary green color to form a color spectrum for each season." These newly created brand elements are applied to all elements of communication and in-store design.

In keeping with the new logo and visual communication design, a new retail concept was established. Katschinski says:

> *This new concept wants customers to find themselves in a loft apartment of good friends rather than in a store. To achieve this, we imagined how the interior of the cosmopolitan jetsetter's apartment would be arranged. Also, the incorporation of the central theme—"Cosmopolitan Jetsetters"—needed to be translated into a universal store concept.*

To achieve the desired effect gigantic suitcases were introduced as displayers and they also suggest the wanderlust and "world travelers" idea of the brand theme. Also, reintroduced were the new logo patterns that now line the suitcase interiors and appear as wallpaper in the dressing rooms. Above the cash desk "the visual of the actual Monton campaign was installed." Maintaining the desired loft-look are the floor screed, white metal, and the open ceilings with a metal light system that "contributes to the stylish, minimalistic approach and guarantees maximum flexibility." Katschinski adds: "Through the mannequins (that appear on the floor) the overall brand appearance is accentuated. They do form an important aspect of the general idea. In tandem with the loft concept, they represent a modern and simplistic look—underlining the image of 'jetsetters'."

CONCLUSION

The new brand identity, as created by the dan pearlman organization in close cooperation with Monton, opened in St. Petersburg, Tallinn, Riga, Vilnius, and Krasnodar and will be adapted to future Monton stores as well. As Volker Katschinski sums it up, "It's about awakening the spirit for discovery and having fun: contrasting colors, souvenirs from around the world, and a selection of design classics that invite you to become part of the community of Cosmopolitan Jetsetters."

DESIGN CREDITS:

Design:	dan pearlman Markenarchitektur, Berlin, Germany
	Concept (Retail): Volker Katschinski: Creative Director/Founder
	Concept (VC): Jork Andre Dieter
Client:	Monton
Photography:	Aivo Kallas at Kliff Klaus / Courtesy of Monton

◀ **Figure 1:** To upgrade the Monton brand it was important to make the visual identity and new store design appealing to the wider market. The new double stripe flag logo appears with the store name above the open entrance to the shop.

◀ **Figure 2:** Appealing to young men and women is the new tagline "Cosmopolitan Jetsetters." Here—in "Monton country"—the shop is like a loft apartment shared with friends.

▶ **Figure 3:** The interior is arranged as one imagines a cosmopolitan jetsetter would live. Giant suitcases serve as display fixtures to suggest wanderlust and world travel.

▶ **Figure 4:** A wall fixture—in the "travel" concept–that is an oversized abstraction of a steamer trunk laid open to display the assorted outfits. The weathered, gray-toned timber floor and open ceilings maintain the loft look.

◀ **Figure 5:** The neutral palette continues into the dressing area where draw curtains provide privacy and seating is provided for friends who wait.

◀ **Figure 6:** A giant illuminated wall of monitors features graphics of the Cosmopolitan Jetsetters who shop at Monton. The cash/wrap desk carries the Monton name and flag logo.

CASE STUDY 2.7

SOLARA

CARREFOUR RICHELIEU, SAINT-JEAN-SUR-RICHELIEU, QUEBEC, CANADA

DESIGN: RUSCIO STUDIO, MONTREAL, CANADA

DESIGN OBJECTIVE

What do you do when the brand name is not an ideal fit with the product or the image you would like to present? You can't change it—but you can certainly enhance it. That was the first challenge faced by Robert Ruscio, president of the Ruscio Studio in Montreal, when called upon to upscale the look of the Solara shoe store to make it more suitable—make it fit in with its neighbors in the Carrefour Richelieu. The previous two Solara shops were, as Robert Ruscio stated, "flavorless and bland" with "white walls, white melamine shelves, light gray tiles, and wall-to-wall merchandise." In addition, the name Solara seemed better suited to a space selling sun shades or for a tanning salon.

DESIGN SOLUTION

Ruscio continues: "The store needed distinction. The client needed to laser-in, rather than cast a wide net and speak to a precise target market. As the company name could not be changed, the next best option was to come up with a tag line. 'Sois éblouissante!' (Be dazzling!) was added and appears under the name both at the storefront and on the rear counter wall, making the name much more relevant to the offerings." Also, the client was concerned that the new stylish and upgraded look of the shop would defeat a very important aspect of his brand—value pricing. The solution was to add the bold statement "La mode a bas prix" (Fashion at value prices) on a large floor unit up near the storefront. "The message is visually clear to all passers-by and reaffirms the store's brand position."

The storefront had to open up based on the store's average price points but the double-door entrance "was purely suggestive of a more exclusive price offering." Along with the wide-open façade there is an angled wall upon which the latest in shoe trends are introduced. The rear wall of the shop, with its full-height wall graphic that can readily be seen from the mall aisle, becomes part of the store's façade. The graphic, the black background, and the store logo also serves as a balance between the left and right walls, one being predominantly white with indirect lighting, the other having a golden background with white linear shelving.

Ruscio explains that since the company does not have a visual department that produces regularly scheduled program changes, "We developed visuals that were more permanent, bolder, reflective of the lifestyle target market and appropriate for every season. The limited but bold visuals zero in on a specific demographic and more accurately reflect the merchandise offerings." Also, he adds, "The new color palette of white, black, and gold offers the perfect combination that reflects the brand's new attributes—women, fashion, and trendy."

Upon entering the space, the shopper cannot but be aware of the "shoe cloud ceiling"—a fantasy created with over 6500 women's shoes finished in glossy white. In a way, this unique effect was an answer to the client's question about what to do with overstocked products that eventually become a "dead inventory." Since the client didn't actually have enough "dead inventory," he was forced to buy up his competitors' residual stock. "The unique 'shoe cloud ceiling' is also an expression of creativity and originality for the Solara brand. It is a visual effect that is surreal and yet not visually overwhelming. It is fun, audacious, and unique. The visual focuses on a particular demographic group and makes the store more appealing from the mall. Everyone walking by the store has a reaction or comment to make." A mirror on the top of the right wall creates an illusion of more store width as the shoe cloud seems to appear beyond the golden wall display panel on the wall.

In order to have greater flexibility in merchandising, the designers introduced three systems. A floating shelving system with odd shaped shelves appears on the right wall while on the left wall, higher-end products are highlighted and illuminated on shelves supported by a custom backlit outrigger system. Various collections are presented on two black floor units featuring moveable rectangular tabletop platforms. Ruscio adds: "The end of each unit discreetly incorporates a charcoal leather bench, adding style to this grand unit. By introducing only two 14 ft display tables in the entire space, the store was decluttered and a bold statement was made." Breaking up the perimeter walls are special feature sections. Handbags appear on the left wall, hanging on golden metal pegs against hexagonal mirror plates. The new arrivals—"Nouveautés!"—are on view on the right wall.

In summing up, Robert Ruscio says:

With the original store concept, the emphasis was placed mostly on value pricing. In the new concept—the new brand identity—equal importance is placed on trendy fashion. Also, by creating sections for the different categories, there is a greater value that is added to the same product as the customer can browse more easily.

CONCLUSION

The results have more than satisfied the client who is now planning to apply this new brand identity in his existing stores and expand out with it into other regional AA malls. The design has also won several auspicious awards including an ARE Retail Design Award for Innovative Visual Presentation and the ICSC's Maple Leaf Silver Award for "Retail Store Design Excellence."

DESIGN CREDITS:

Design:	Ruscio Studio, Montreal, QC, Canada Robert Ruscio: President Charles-Antoine Montpetit: Creative Director Catherine Landry: Project Manager
Client:	Solara Ralph Chouha: President
Photography:	Leeza Studio

◀ **Figure 1:** The sharp contrast between the black façade and the glistening white interior indicates the store's new sophisticated identity, and the double-door entrance "is purely suggestive of a more exclusive price offering."

◀ **Figure 2:** Though the Solara brand identity is upscaled, the message boldly stated up front ("Fashion at value prices") "is visually clear to all passers-by and reaffirms the store's brand position."

▶ **Figure 3:** Making an immediate impact—from the mall aisle and upon entering the shop—is the shoe cloud ceiling made from over 6500 women's shoes finished in glossy white.

▲ **Figure 4:** The mirror, near the black back wall, creates the illusion of more space and the shoe cloud, made up of "dead inventory," appears to go on endlessly.

◀ **Figure 5:** Featured items appear on the two 14 ft fixtures that stand in mid-store. They "declutter" the merchandise presentation and "make a bold statement." Each unit ends with charcoal leather benches that add style to these grand units.

CASE STUDY 2.8

BARBICAN

BARBICAN CENTRE, LONDON, UK

DESIGN: SHH ARCHITECTS, LONDON, UK

DESIGN OBJECTIVE

The Barbican Centre is a world-class brand in arts and performance and the Barbican buildings are distinctive landmarks in London's varied architecture. The architects and designers at SHH Architects of London were challenged to create a food hall and a lounge that would, according to Neil Hogan, SHH's Creative Director, "bring this Centre's food and beverage offer up to the level of the Barbican's long-established worldwide reputation for art exhibitions and performances." The concept was to create two new environments that would become destination places in their own right.

DESIGN SOLUTION

Neil Hogan continues: "We had to create an identity for each space and a range of brand applications that didn't comprise the long-established identity of the Barbican Centre, but which were also strong enough to communicate a stand-alone vision." As the interior and branding designer of the project, SHH had to turn the former 450 sq. meter (approx. 4840 sq. ft) ground-floor cafe into a restaurant/food shop now rebranded as Barbican Foodhall, and the first-floor bar/restaurant into the Barbican Lounge. Both spaces included outdoor terraces. To accomplish the transformation, Neil Hogan explains, "The answer was to dare to be simple—introducing capitalization for impact but staying clearly related to the Centre's lower-case identity before adding the building itself as a minimalist icon for brand applications, including point of sale, menus, coasters, take-away cups, bags, and a 'bag for life'. Getting the relationship right between the existing building and brand was crucial—establishing 'playful yet respectful' links between the two generations of design."

> *Our overall approach was to link the spaces back to the wonderful architecture of the Barbican itself and celebrate the building's materiality by exposing the original concrete ceilings, de-cladding the hammered aggregate walls in the Barbican Lounge space and using Cradley brick pavers for the Foodhall flooring. This not only brought the flooring back in line with the original treatment, but linked it to all the existing Barbican walkways. Our second major*

direction was to create visual connections between the two offers, particularly via the outdoor terraces, which extend from each space. This was achieved partly through planting, but mostly the design of huge, eye-catching and bespoke-designed umbrellas or "urban trees," made of two off-center perforated aluminum disks, with the bottom disk measuring 3 meters (over 9 ft) in width, set into wooden bases, which house both planting and integrated seating.

To animate the spaces, specific details and materials were introduced—like the peacock-green resin floor in the Lounge that matched the color of the water in photos taken of the Barbican outdoor lake in the summer. The new identity for the Foodhall used black and white photographic building icons and "seeks to sit within the current Barbican brand family," although uniquely differentiated by the use of capital rather than traditional lower-case lettering. Handmade and custom steelwork slots, based on the information card slots on the front of Victorian architectural plan chests, and a rolling blackboard used as a daily notice board were part of the point-of-sale information in the Foodhall. "The identity work is cool, crisp, and understated and largely in black and white with measured injections of color." As an example of the light touch that was needed, Robin Day's black polo chairs were used on the terrace of the Barbican Lounge. Hogan explains that Robin Day was the original art director of the Barbican back in 1972 and "we wanted to pay our respects to him, without being in danger of taking the project down memory lane. Here and throughout, it was important to respect the Barbican's structure and history, but also to create a fresh and unified scheme which makes its own truly contemporary statement for now and for years to come."

CONCLUSION

Sir Nicholas Kenyon, Managing Director of the Barbican Centre, said: "We're really excited about the transformation of our food offering. The space has been stripped right back to the original wall textures and fittings, so it really feels like a natural and organic development of our iconic Centre. We're confident regular visitors to the Centre will enjoy the new experience and that this transformation will also help to introduce new people to the area."

DESIGN CREDITS:

Design:	SHH Architects, London, UK Neil Hogan: Creative Director Priya Patel: Branding
Client:	Levy Restaurants Roy Westwood: Creative Director The Barbican Centre
Planting and Gardens:	Kate Gould
Lighting Design:	.PSLAB, Beirut, Lebanon
Photography:	Gareth Gardner (interior views) Caroline Collett (branding and details)

◀ **Figure 1:** The Barbican Centre is situated on the River Thames and has a worldwide reputation for art exhibitions and theatrical presentations. The designers had to create a new identity for the food service areas and the outdoor terraces that each featured.

◀ **Figure 2:** The Barbican Foodhall, located at ground level, is an informal restaurant and take-out service. In the minimalistic design, it is a "playful yet respectful" link with the building's architecture.

◀ Figure 3: The original building's materials are recognized in the concrete ceilings, the hammered aggregate walls and the brick pavers that cover the floor and tie in with the original Barbican walkways. Slender, elegant metal and wood fixtures serve as display cases and area dividers.

◤ **Figure 4:** The Terrace on the upper level is distinguished by the plantings and the "urban trees"— specially designed sun umbrellas. The view of the Thames, the historic buildings, and the new skyline all make this a desirable place to be.

◣ **Figure 5:** The Bar and Lounge on the upper level retains the original concrete ceilings and aggregate walls, while simple drop lights add to the minimalist design of the space. The peacock-green resin floor matches the color of the Barbican lake in the summertime.

▲ **Figure 6:** The Lounge dining area is aglow from the custom lighting reflected in the highly reflective floor. Simple, light metal and wood chairs, accented in red, complement the wood-topped tables, and the glass separator panels are flooded with red light.

CASE STUDY 2.9

OAKVILLE GROCERY

OAKVILLE, NAPA VALLEY, CALIFORNIA, USA

DESIGN: AVILA DESIGN, BERKELEY, CALIFORNIA, USA

DESIGN OBJECTIVE

How do you recreate the brand identity of a business that has been functioning from the same spot, in the same sagging and fatigued structure for over 130 years? The answer is: carefully—lovingly—and with the greatest respect for tradition, heritage, and the goodwill that has been built up over the years. When Leslie Rudd took over the ownership of the Oakville Grocery on St. Helena Highway in the town of Oakville in the Napa Valley, he also acquired a big chunk of history and an icon in this part of California. After all, it is the oldest continually operating store in the state. It has been an essential stop on the highway where tourists can stop for sandwiches, drinks, or essential picnic needs as well as providing the locals with their necessities and also serving as the local post office.

In his brief to the design team of Avila Design, Leslie Rudd asked that "the customer experience be improved: more queuing space to order sandwich and deli items, more circulation space for viewing merchandise and more paying stations—but the integrity of the store had to be respected."

DESIGN SOLUTION

Dusan Motolik, Project Manager and Designer at Avila Design, had another problem: the age and condition of the old building itself. "It was agreed that the building needed some attention. We had a dilemma: it needed serious repair—it was unsafe—it didn't work as a store, but Leslie Rudd wanted to preserve it as it was. We were supposed to preserve the building for the next 100 years." Thus, the owner and the designer decided to keep it as close to the original as possible—"to retain all that unique character—to remember it as it was."

The architectural rehabbing of the building was extensive with an effort made throughout to save or salvage as much of the original as possible— to keep the same feel, texture, and material quality of the antique grocery. People who stop and shop at the Oakville Grocery still see the vintage soft drink billboard painted on the side of the building; the original corrugated "tin" roofing is still there though it now rests over a waterproofed roof structure; and the welcoming shaded porch still is supported by posts that are still out of plumb. Dusan Motolik explains:

"Traditional design, materials, and construction methods were critical to the branding message of Oakville Grocery. The hand skills of carpenters, masons, and cabinet makers were engaged to put the store back in order." The uneven worn oak floor was ripped up and replaced by a new saw tail oak floor that was installed over a structural concrete slab. The original painted wood-bead board ceiling remained untouched along with the mismatched collection of vintage lighting fixtures. Local craftspeople, using traditional fabrication methods, created the merchandising fixtures using re-milled stock from reclaimed Douglas fir railroad ties, while the vintage wood and glass cooler doors were reused; the walk-in cooler was upgraded for energy efficiency. Motolik adds: "The colors and textures inside the store are the honest materials themselves: the rich brown of natural oak and Douglas fir, the crisp white of Carrara marble counters, the enduring classicism of fresh white paint."

To accommodate Leslie Rudd's brief, the post office was relocated to another part of the site and a coffee bar was set up to serve drinks, ice cream, and locally prepared pastries. A long wall of shelving was created with pop-out shelves for product tasting stations, and, as in the original store layout, the deli was arranged as an island. To ease the crowding that can occur inside, a new Dutch-door service window was opened to the front porch.

As part of the new/old rebranding, the original rabbit logo was kept but the graphics were updated. Laura Riggs, a designer on this project, adds: "Bags, labels, cups now hark back to an earlier era of postal rubber stamps and brown paper sacks, local seasonal produce and a business which also serves as a center for a rural community." The store now also features self-labeled mustards, spreads, wines, and assorted condiments and products, mainly from the Sonoma and Napa Valley, along with locally grown fresh produce.

CONCLUSION

Dusan Motolik says: "From the client's initial impulse to preserve a piece of history that could be lost forever, through the careful historic restoration, to the graphic branding and the new merchandise, the Oakville Grocery strengthened its brand by strengthening its customers' emotional tie to the past, preparing for the future 100 years."

DESIGN CREDITS:

Design:	Avila Design, Berkeley, California, USA David Avila: Principal Dusan Motolik: Project Manager/Lead Designer Laura Riggs: Designer Calvin Tam: Job Captain
Client:	Leslie Rudd, Oakville Grocery Guy Byrne: Client's Project Manager
General Contractor:	Island Construction
Millwork:	Rudd Construction
Photography:	Wilson Lee Photography, Clovis, California, USA. © 2012 Wilson Lee Photography

◀ **Figure 1:** The "oldest continually operating store in California" looks today as it did over 130 years ago—only stronger and customer improved. The Oakville Grocery still serves locals and tourists passing on the highway.

◀ **Figure 2:** Hand-skilled carpenters, masons, and cabinet makers put the store back into working order and looking "old" but still up to date. "Traditional design, materials, and construction methods were critical to the branding message of the Oakville Grocery."

◀ **Figure 3:** The original painted wood-bead ceiling and the mismatched vintage lighting fixtures were retained while new floor fixtures were made from reclaimed Douglas fir railroad ties. The deli section is now an island again, as it was in the original plan.

◀ **Figure 4:** The new coffee bar also serves ice cream and locally prepared pastries. The new design "retains all the unique character" of the old-time grocery—"to remember it as it was."

◀ **Figure 5:** A forgotten hand-dug well was discovered when the original floor was ripped up to fit the new structural concrete slab that was installed under the new wood floor. The top of that abandoned brick well is illuminated and covered over with glass and is a reminder of the 1881 original store.

▶ **Figure 6:** The walk-in cooler was upgraded for energy efficiency but the wood, glass, and hardware of the original door were reused to effect a "unique merchandiser for cold drinks."

CASE STUDY 2.10

SANDBAR

ANNA MARIA ISLAND, FLORIDA, USA

DESIGN: THE SCHIMBERG GROUP, SARASOTA, FLORIDA, USA

DESIGN OBJECTIVE

Sometimes an old, established, and much beloved brand needs gentle tweaking to make it more acceptable to a new audience while still holding firm to what the brand has always represented. Way back in 1949, two old army barracks replaced a now destroyed bathhouse to become the Sandbar Restaurant on Anna Maria Island on the Gulf of Mexico in Florida. Over the years there were numerous changes made to the restaurant but, according to Barron Schimberg, Principal of the Schimberg Group, "it always stayed true to its roots—a rustic, neighborhood place that locals and tourists alike found to be home. It always represented delicious fresh food, good company, and glorious sunsets. It was always, and continues to this day, to be about the view."

Ed Chiles of the Chiles Restaurant Group wanted and needed to update the Sandbar for the twenty-first century. Most important to him and the Sandbar's many faithful patrons was that the renovation "maintain the essence of the place." The Schimberg Group was invited to bring out that "essence" and challenged to gently modernize the structure and the brand.

DESIGN SOLUTION

Barron Schimberg says: "The Sandbar is about authenticity and not losing the essence of its history. The restaurant is about views, water, and comfort. We took what was old and reinvented it to be new and fresh, but never left the roots of why people loved the restaurant in the first place—its rustic beginnings." He goes on to explain that the design team "strategically blended contemporary with rustic design: modern fabric patterns with dark wood chairs; a shabby chic wood ceiling hovering over a sisal-look, modern Chilewich floor system; painted beach pail light fixtures with antique bulbs to provide light over a terrazzo-poured bar top." In addition, architecturally, the designers relocated the entrance: it now greets diners with a breathtaking view of the Gulf. The bar was relocated so that patrons actually face the beach rather than a mirrored wall. The dining booths were raised off the dining room floor and oriented in an east/west direction so that diners can get an unobstructed view of the fabulous sunsets. And, Barron Schimberg points out, "Most creatively, a feature wall made of refurbished Anna Maria Island pier wood is highlighted with strips of antiqued mirrors—allowing customers and employees to have glimpses of the water, no matter where they may be in the restaurant." Add the 15 ft high vaulted ceiling with large timber construction and the 5 ft tall windows that appear throughout—there is always a view.

CONCLUSION

Patty Schimberg, Principal and Interior Design Director, sums it up:

> *The brand concept was very clear from the get go. Finding the perfect light fixtures—repurposed mason jars and sand pails—using elements of local significance like pier ties and terrazzo, finding the color palette that just "fit in" to the stunning beach the restaurant sits on—not to take away from it (or worse, match it)—these were enormously important choices for our design team. It's still the Sandbar—an already successful, living legend—and, since the renovations, it really feels better, yet still familiar. It's one of those projects that remind us what we love about our work.*

Probably the greatest compliment is that patrons—old and new—say, "It's just like the original restaurant—but better." The brand stands—just a bit more upright.

DESIGN CREDITS:

Design:	The Schimberg Group, Sarasota, Florida, USA Barron Schimberg, AIA: Principal and Architect Patty Schimberg: Principal and Interior Designer
Client:	Ed Chiles of the Chiles Restaurant Group
Contractor:	Whitehead Construction
Photography:	Greg Wilson Photography. © Greg Wilson 2010

▲ **Figure 1:** What once was two old World War II army barracks has evolved into the new, gracious but still familiar Sandbar Restaurant. The newly relocated entrance offers patrons a view of the Gulf of Mexico.

◀ **Figure 2:** Rather than facing a mirrored wall, patrons at the bar have a view out to the water and the sunsets. The terrazzo-topped bar is a "design element of local significance."

◀ **Figure 3:** Beyond the semi-transparent divider wall accented with wine bottles is the spacious dining area. The high vaulted ceiling with timber trusses adds an open yet warm, comforting quality to the design.

◀ **Figure 4:** The booths are raised up off the dining room floor so that diners can enjoy a view of the water and the sunsets. The modern fabric pattern was selected to complement the seaside setting rather than compete or blend in with it.

▶ Figure 5: The feature wall combines refurbished wood from the Anna Maria Island pier accented with antiqued mirror strips affording views of the seas from anywhere in the dining room. It combines local history with the brand's identity.

CASE STUDY 2.11

DORMA

THE BAU FAIR, MUNICH, GERMANY

DESIGN: DAN PEARLMAN MARKENARCHITEKTUR, BERLIN, GERMANY

DESIGN OBJECTIVE

DORMA is noted for its automatic door controls, moveable walls, glass fittings, and security and access controls and, as they proclaim on their website, DORMA is "a reliable global partnership for premium access solutions and services that better buildings allow." They have been a recognized leader in the industry for over a century but now felt it was time for a new brand identity. With core principles like "innovation and quality" and brand values stressing aestheticism and design, it needed the designers to look ahead and come up with a new brand identity that is "From Today to Tomorrow."

DESIGN SOLUTION

Professor Marcus Fischer and the design team of the dan pearlman Markenarchitektur design firm of Berlin were challenged to create that identity—to be introduced in the form of a trade show stand at the BAU Fair in Munich. Marcus Fischer explains: "DORMA was a new client to the portfolio of dan pearlman. Therefore, the overall preparation was much more detailed in comparison to an already known client. The first step in approaching the project was to understand the already established brand from scratch. What are its values, its mission, and the competitive advantages? Only when these aspects were understood and a general feeling for the brand could be developed was it possible to create a booth that reflected the brand's identity by means of using architecture and design." In connection to the re-launch and rejuvenation of the brand DORMA, the trade fair stand was established. The brand values of quality, innovation, design and aesthetics, and a problem-free and holistic approach formed the basis of the presentation.

The new DORMA brand identity showing a strengthened focus on innovation was introduced at the BAU Fair in Munich. Marcus Fischer continues: "In order to reflect the brand thoroughly, the team of dan pearlman had to consider DORMA's signature colors, the logo, and other characteristics which all together form the brand identity. The approach of dan pearlman's experience architecture was to imagine, 'If DORMA was a human being what would be its characteristics, how would it look?' In this way a special atmosphere was created around the brand, being reflected in the trade fair stand. Key visual elements connected to the brand formed the basis for the architectural design. In this way partners, guests, and employees were warmly welcomed to the new world of DORMA."

Based on the idea of a housewarming party, the keywords in respect to the visitor were *warm*, *welcoming*, and *personal*. The same idea was applied to the "look and feel" of the trade fair stand. Within the center of the stand's total of 670 sq. meters (approx. 7200 sq. ft) the brand wall let the booth come to life. The brand wall introduced the world of DORMA by means of innovative multimedia technology and the screening of the brand reel. "With the underlying idea in mind, the architects and interior designers of dan pearlman chose the appearance and characteristics of a house as their inspiration. The white, layered levels express coziness while expressing aesthetic and qualitative standards at the same time. Overall the layout is open and inviting, with an intuitive guidance system for the visitor." From the brand wall, the path then continues through the installation, passing a display of the latest DORMA products as well as the catering area, before reaching the stairs to the first floor. Here, guests find themselves in the "innovation box" area, which offers them an exclusive look at DORMA's new products and their developmental process.

Fischer says:

> *Establishing the trade fair stand at the BAU 2013, which is recognized as one of the leading fairs for architects, materials, and systems, was only the first step in order to complete a whole new spatial concept and showroom with an entirely new design language. When rolling out a project with international relevance like the DORMA trade fair stand, it is essential to keep in mind that the design should be applicable internationally. It is important to make sure that any symbols, colors, projections, etc. apply to the cultural and ethical rules of the specific environment. Likewise, possible changes to the corporate design must mean that there are no crucial adaptations that change the recognition value.*

CONCLUSION

With core principles like "innovation and quality" and brand values of "effortlessness, holism, design, and aestheticism," the design team, under the leadership of Marcus Fischer, created the trade show stand using clear cubic forms. They created the prize-winning, open, and inviting space that relayed the "Design the 360 degree experience" that the DORMA corporation requested. Design and functionality became one in this space and created the new DORMA brand identity—"From Today to Tomorrow."

DESIGN CREDITS:

Design:	dan pearlman Markenarchitektur, Berlin, Germany Marcus Fischer: Designer Moritz von Voss: Executive Architect
Client:	DORMA
Exhibition Stand Construction:	setcubed
Communication:	Dentsu McGarry Bowen
Product Communication:	GRAMM
Photography:	Karsten Rabas

▲ **Figure 1:** DORMA's signature colors of red and white and its logo are immediately evident to the visitor. Based on the concept of a housewarming party, the designers created a warm and welcoming feel in the vast space.

▶ **Figure 2:** The welcome desk is on the right, along with the stairs leading to the upper level. Above it is the brand wall, featuring multimedia technology to introduce the revitalized brand. The red overhead panel carries the brand's promise for the future along with the established logo.

▶ **Figure 3:** Beyond the tiered seating where visitors meet and are entertained is a dining/work area, almost all white and accented in DORMA red.

▲ **Figure 4:** Entertainment is a must and in the theater tucked away under the balcony the spotlight is on showmanship. Live performances as well as videos entertain and educate the visitors.

◀ **Figure 5:** Flanking the staircase to the upper level is a wall of framed DORMA product images. It serves as an introduction to the "innovation box" where visitors learn about the brand's new products.

▲ **Figure 6:** On the upper level visitors are shown products in development. Clear cubic forms are used throughout and the symbols, colors, and projections are suited to the cultural and ethical rules of the environment.

PART 3

A Brand Travels

CASE STUDIES

Part of being a successful brand is having the ability to expand, stretch, and move out into new areas, new cities, new countries and cultures. Although we say "it's a small world," it is still large enough for people to speak different languages and have special customs and beliefs. Even colors can mean different things to different people. Thus, when a brand decides to move out and enter new or foreign markets, it means learning about that market and how to make the brand welcome and accepted. The brands in this section have all "moved out"—some have moved only to a different part of the country, others have skipped over oceans and borders to get the brand accepted.

Galeries Lafayette, when they opened in Jakarta in Indonesia, emphasized the Frenchness of the brand because that is what the upwardly mobile shoppers in Jakarta want and expect. France—and Paris in particular—still stands as the epitome of fashion in Indonesia and the Asia-Pacific region, and thus Paris and its architecture and its icons fill the new store. There is even an abstract Eiffel Tower, which proudly dominates the main floor of Galeries Lafayette, while graphic elements of Beaux-Arts architecture appear throughout. A visit to this department store is like "one day in Paris" without leaving home.

In a similar way, **Wrangler** in Leipzig, Germany plays up the American West with subtle decorative touches. Denims and jeans are so very American; thus the brand makes its appeal by emphasizing Wrangler's raw and rustic past. The raw and rustic appeal is in the materials and textures used, while the stenciled Navajo rug and faded stars-and-stripes fabric used in the dressing rooms are witnesses to the American West, as are the pony skin covered chairs. "Small world" comment: A British design firm designed the store in Germany that promotes "the original American outdoor brand."

Allen Solly in Bangalore, India is British in attitude and texture for the professional Indian men and women who shop there. Maybe there is still some long-ago memory in the minds of upwardly mobile Indian professionals that regards things British as things to be desired or attained. This formerly British owned, now Indian owned, chain of stores presents its Britishness with the material palette, the custom tartan fabric, and the antlered stag head that recalls the heritage and tradition of the original English firm.

Though **Maidenform** has, during its more than 90-year history, built strong equity for the brand and become well known throughout North America, some European countries, and even China, this was to be its first Chilean flagship store and physical entry into Chile. According to the designer/architect, "it needed to be an effective and recognizable design that could transmit the brand's values of sophistication and sensuality and create a strong emotional bond with Chilean customers."

PUMA Osaka proudly shows the brand's color and the leaping puma but adds some decidedly Japanese motifs to make their audience feel more at home with the brand. The design is simple, in keeping with Japanese-style architecture, and is enhanced with elements of Japanese art and culture. There is origami-style seating and, as the designers said, "By including local aspects in the retail design, the brand gives their consumers a feeling that it respects the location, its particularities, and especially the values and demands and desires of the local customers."

Joe Fresh's move across the border from Canada to the United States was hardly a move at all. The designers of the Joe Fresh stores in Canada brought the same flair and architectural drama to the unique structure on Fifth Avenue in Manhattan. Here, the major problem for the Joe Fresh brand was not moving from across the border but staking its place and finding its market on Fifth Avenue amidst so many other well-known brands, all looking to cater to the same young, trendy shoppers—and to accomplish the move into a landmark, modernist building that is almost entirely sheathed in glass. The result is a gallery-like experience that reflects the historical importance of the structure yet presents a brand that is "proudly Canadian."

The **Wawa** chain of convenience stores, in their move into the Florida market from the mid-Atlantic states where they are well known, required making adjustments for the architecture and preferences of that market. Wawa needed a new design that would reflect the Florida location but that would tell the market that this is not your usual convenience store usually attached to a line of gas pumps. Pastel colors, pitched roofs, and a front porch bring the building more into line with its neighborhood while the interior is fresh, open, and new.

When **Whole Foods** opened in Detroit, it didn't bring anything along except its brand values and its name. Otherwise, the store design lives, breathes, and salutes Detroit and all it once stood for. Did ever a design reflect its location and say more clearly "We are here with you"? I doubt it. Textures, materials, and numerous found objects that refer to Detroit's culture and history have been incorporated into the design. The result is a unique market that is part of the community and is "a colorful, eclectic and locally relevant diary of the area's past."

The elements that were used in **Carlo Pazolini** shops in Europe appear in similar forms but adjusted to respect the SoHo space in New York City that the brand now occupies. Though these signature design elements stamp the brand on the space, the designer adapts these elements to reinforce the history of the structure. Thus, each Carlo Pazolini store is reminiscent of other Carlo Pazolini outlets because of the color palette and the strong sweep of sinuous lines and ceiling patterns. However, each is unique in its relationship to its site and the location of the site. The brand travels and its signature elements move along with it.

One of the designs we have included actually does travel. The award-winning **JanSport** kiosk is a movable shop that can be set up in a limited space and folds up when not in use. The fixture is actually a store-in-a-box and can be open and functioning, in a space of 10 feet × 10 feet, in minutes. It represents the brand in a manner consistent with JanSport's full-size retail environments.

A pop-up shop is no longer a "sometimes thing." It is becoming a regular feature in retail design. The ability to move in—and move on out—quickly and efficiently while leaving behind visual images of the brand in the minds of shoppers is what makes the pop-up so valuable to the brand. It is really all about speed and mobility. The **adidas** pop-up shop we have included is one of two created by the Roundhouse design firm for two very different locations but with the same goal in mind. It was not only the adidas brand's identity that was involved in the design; the host store—Urban Outfitters—brand was also carefully nurtured by the designers. We included a view of the second shop so that the reader can see how the essential elements of the concept were carried through in the sunny space.

Though many brands do still replicate their brand's store design as they set themselves down in other locales, the trend now is toward designing stores, like the Whole Foods store, where the community is recognized in the design and the brand becomes a neighbor in the neighborhood. Like the community wall in Domino's and the façade of Medi, the brand moves in and becomes an integral part of the local scene—no matter what language is spoken and what the local customs might be.

CASE STUDY 3.1

GALERIES LAFAYETTE

JAKARTA, INDONESIA

DESIGN: PLAJER & FRANZ STUDIO, BERLIN, GERMANY

DESIGN OBJECTIVE

Mention the name Galeries Lafayette and, to anybody who has visited the fabled city of Paris, it will bring back visions of a breathtaking, century-old, ten-story Beaux-Arts building near the Palais Garnier opera house, with its stained glass and steel domed ceiling, art nouveau staircases, and the wealth of high-end designer and internationally famous fashion brands contained within. How do you take this famous department store and bring it to another continent—another culture, another "world"—and yet maintain and enhance the brand that has stood for high fashion and good taste for so long?

The design had to appear as French as possible and play up the mother store's Parisian setting because the shopper, though in Jakarta, had to feel as though he or she was in the French Palace of Fashion. Yet, for all its smart and sophisticated fashionable French attitude and the abstract Eiffel Tower on the main floor, the store's design had to be accessible and comfortable for the Indonesian shoppers and be a part of the place where it is located.

DESIGN SOLUTION

According to Alexander Plajer, CEO and co-founder of plajer & franz studio, the Berlin-based design firm that designed the new Galeries Lafayette in Pacific Place—"the up and coming place in Jakarta"—the designing process begins with gathering information about the client and the brand: "Information is crucial. Today, a store concept is about reflecting the DNA of the brand including its character, heritage, its spirit, its vision and mission. In addition to meeting with the client, we also do our own individual research to learn about the external effect of the brand and the way it is perceived. It is important to find out where the brand is positioned and who is the competition—as well as know the brand's communication." The firm's approach to designing a department store follows. "Here we have a stand-alone brand—a department store—and filled with multiple sub-brands with diverse individual images, characters, and visual appearances." He explains that rather than only the DNA of the department store dominating the look, or those of the sub-brands taking over, *we need to find a way in which all the brands remain autonomous while being integrated into a single unit. Thus, when you enter the department store in Jakarta, you will immediately receive the feeling of being in Galeries Lafayette, the fashion temple with a decidedly French heritage. And yet, the sub-brands have their own presence. The department store brand should create a frame for the sub-brands. You can compare it with a painting, with the impact it has on the frame. A well-chosen frame does not detract from the content of the painting; it emphasizes it while being visible and presenting itself as well. Since a department store is diverse and huge in size, it not only needs to take over the "framing" role, but also give re-emerging focus points to create a consumer journey and help customers find their way—and very importantly—keep the customer's interest during the visit.*

The 12,000 sq. meter (approx. 126,700 sq. ft) building houses over 300 international brands on four floors. There is never any doubt that the shopper is in a French store. The brand's DNA is all about being and exuding French style. Plajer explains: "The leitmotif of the design concept is 'One day in Paris', and the unrivaled flair of the French capital is visible and sensed in every corner of the store. Typical Parisian elements such as building façades and the Eiffel Tower are interpreted in an accessible but warm way." The famous glass and steel dome in the Paris store "reappears as an over-sized ceiling and lighting element on all four floors, marking the crossing points between various segments and highlighting the DNA of the brand." Appearing on some of the double-sided indoor partitions, which are made of sandblasted glass and mirrors, are "sketchy motifs of Parisian building façades and street lamps. These 'walls' serve to separate different brands from each other and in this way create a kind of display window for each of them. Red—one of the colors of Galeries Lafayette—draws a continuous line throughout the entire department store, making its strongest statement in the Eiffel Tower." A modern interpretation of that noted Parisian landmark is used as a strong vertical element next to the stairway near the entrance into the store. As Alexander Plajer explains, "The landmark of the French capital enjoys great prestige in Asia and creates highly esteemed value."

When asked how important the sensory cues are when bringing the very French Galeries Lafayette to Jakarta, Plajer replies: "This strongly depends upon the character of the brand. A store design wants to approach customers on an emotional level, hence it usually includes certain sensory aspects. These can include materials, colors, surfaces as well as aromas and music. They are part of the brand's identity and its communication with its consumers. Sensory cues have to match the character of the brand and type of merchandise it offers. It should also respect the local relevance of where the store is located and what is the brand's origin. Of course, serving colorful macaroons in a 'Marie Antoinette French-style fashion boutique' could be a great asset to the shopping experience in a non-French situated shop."

CONCLUSION

Summing up the contribution of plajer & franz's design efforts, Plajer said: "The store architecture creates a scene for the product and the brand—Galeries Lafayette. Its DNA, identity, mission, and vision are all put to the fore while setting a framework for the multiple and diverse sub-brands." This is a situation where we can say "Let them eat macaroons"—and know the shoppers will enjoy it.

DESIGN CREDITS:

Architecture and Interior Design:	plajer & franz studio, Berlin, Germany Alexander Plajer: CEO and Co-Founder
Client:	Galeries Lafayette
Local Architect:	DIP Consult, Jakarta, Indonesia
Shopfitting:	Haras, Indonesia
Lighting:	ansorg
Photography:	Ken Schluctmann /diephotodesigner.de

◀ **Figure 1:** "Come spend a day in Paris while never leaving Jakarta!" That was the design concept behind bringing the essence of the very Parisian department store brand to the upwardly mobile market of Jakarta.

◀ **Figure 2:** Using warm and rich colors and materials, the designers "created a modern fashion temple that reflects the mix-and-match philosophy of the Galeries Lafayette brand." Wide boulovard aisles and kiosk-like fixtures help create the Paris feel.

◀ **Figure 3:** Oversized ceiling and lighting elements on all four floors mark the crossing point between various segments and highlight the DNA of the brand. Shown here is the main level and the Cosmetics area.

◀ **Figure 4:** A modern interpretation of the Eiffel Tower appears in a giant floor-to-high-ceiling skeletal construction near the elevators on the ground level. It is Mondrianesque in design, with some open spaces filled with either product display or panels of red.

◀ **Figure 5:** A front-on view of the modern interpretation of the Eiffel Tower, which adds a very strong Parisian touch to the interior design.

◀ **Figure 6:** Artwork panels with Parisian architectural details appear as dividers or focal elements throughout the store, again underlining the French brand. Here they frame the Lingerie shop.

◀ **Figure 7:** Toujour l'amour—and always the glamour of Paris. Gilded abstract mannequins and swooping crystal chandeliers add a luxurious and theatrical touch to the Formal Wear area. Soft drapery and the tufted pouf seating all add to the Frenchness of the brand.

◀ **Figure 8:** Dark woods add to the look of the Men's department. The "coupole" or dome—a signature element in the Paris store—appears at these marked crossings in the plan as a lighting feature over a focal display stage.

CASE STUDY 3.2

WRANGLER

LEIPZIG, GERMANY

DESIGN: CHECKLAND KINDLEYSIDES, LONDON, UK

DESIGN OBJECTIVE

Charlie Hudson founded the Hudson Overall Company over a century ago but the name Wrangler—a term used for a working cowboy—did not come into use until 1947 when the company began producing jeans for cowboys. Today, its heritage as the "original American outdoor denim brand" is unrivaled. On its website the brand proclaims: "Wrangler jeans are built for strength and tailored for freedom. Wearing Wrangler jeans, we can surrender to animal instincts, embrace the rush of adrenaline, and be our natural, wild, spontaneous selves."

For its first store in Germany, in Leipzig, Wrangler called upon the design talents of the Checkland Kindleysides design consultancy of London. The design brief was to "capture the spirit of the Wrangler brand," says Jeff Kindleysides, Creative Director. "Conceptually the store needed to feel impulsive and industrious; this is important for a brand like Wrangler that is full of adrenaline. We also wanted to capture the notion that Wrangler jeans are 'built for strength and tailored for freedom' and again this comes through in the finished store design." The store had to recreate the feeling of the American West for the German market.

DESIGN SOLUTION

Kindleysides explains:

> *Specifically this store is about echoing the past in a contemporary way. Wrangler is an American heritage brand with lots of history and a rawness that is inherent in the denim. This needed to be translated into the store architecture. Cultural references are made to America throughout, from the faded stars and stripes (used as dressing room closures) and the Navajo spray-stenciled rugs, to a palette that is a raw mix of concrete, reclaimed wood, and glass—with a hint at a manufacturing facility.*

The choice of materials and the way they were used "creates an aesthetic which reflects this attitude, from the inherent strength of aged steel to the creation of a skylight and use of glass throughout the store which provide a feeling of translucency that Wrangler is 'the original American outdoor denim brand'."

"The store is laid out with the same consideration to the product range and the consumer. There is clear navigation to the stock for Wrangler's die-hard customers, looking to replenish their favorite/existing styles (generally placed further back in the store), whilst new product and collections attracting the new and fashion-conscious shoppers are placed at the front of the store." Up front is the denim drawing table that is accentuated by the "Navajo rug" that has been stenciled on the concrete floor. Here, Wrangler's newest key items are presented. The "factory window" frames appear throughout and "create a flexible graphic mosaic where each pane can have a different character; some are plain, tarnished, frosted, or mirrored, whilst others carry photos or graphics to create varied and inspiring backdrops" and serve as references to Wrangler's history and iconography. A ladder system—such as one might find in a storage depot—is used as a simple and functional way of presenting the jeans around the store's perimeter walls, while at the back of the shop there is an easy-to-shop denim wall with a navigation system that simplifies shopping for the Wrangler customer looking for his or her favorite jeans. "The bespoke system uses the same hot rolled steel as the 'factory windows,' with shelving that uses a patchwork of timber, including reclaimed boards, in subtle tonal colors. A fit guide, reminiscent of old cinema signage, provides additional navigational assistance. Women's denim is displayed on fit forms and as outfit collections displayed in supporting bays."

Wrangler's American roots are on full display in the unisex fitting rooms where pony skin covered Eames chairs are placed in front of another "factory window" in the open waiting area. The individual reclaimed wood sheathed dressing rooms have stars and stripes flags—over-dyed in black—as closing curtains and a "factory skylight" creates the illusion of natural daylight. Sitting in the center of the shop is the cash desk, designed as an open, steel-framed cage reminiscent of a workshop office, which continues the industrial feel of the design. The enamel machinists' lamps and factory lights also add to the Wrangler heritage feel.

CONCLUSION

Even though this design was created as a prototype to be rolled out in other European cities, according to Jeff Kindleysides it was site specific. "The concept was designed to be modular. With each site we enhance the inherent quality of the building or space, and the system we have produced will flex into any environment. The store design captures the values and origins of the brand in a contemporary setting, with architectural cues providing a backdrop which bring Wrangler's denim to life, resulting in a store experience that is pared back, raw, and effortless to shop."

Franz van Zeeland, President of Wrangler EMEA, says: "Wrangler is about building on the past to shape the future. I think Checkland Kindleysides has done a fantastic job in terms of capturing Wrangler's unique denim heritage. The store is rich in details from Wrangler's past, but it also has a fresh and contemporary feel."

DESIGN CREDITS:

Design:	Checkland Kindleysides, London, UK
	Jeff Kindleysides: Founder Checkland Kindleysides
	Joe Evans: Associate Design Director
	Maggie Wright: Senior Detail Designer
	Victoria Smith: Project Manager
Client:	Wrangler Retail Design Team
	Adam Kakembo: VP Product and Marketing, Wrangler EMEA
	Jeanette Olsen: Trade Marketing Manager, Wrangler EMEA
	Ronnie Borck: Retail Director Jeanswear Europe@ VF Europe
Photography:	Dirk Mathesius / Checkland Kindleysides

▲ **Figure 1:** Bringing the cowboys of the American West to meet the trendy young people of Leipzig in Germany in a retail space that "captured the spirit of the Wrangler brand" was the challenge the architects/designers faced. The solution started in the windows.

◀ **Figure 2:** The design concept underscored the American West, the rawness of the denim, and a hint of the manufacturing facility. The factory lot "window" motif was introduced as a back-up in the open back windows and used throughout the space.

▶ **Figure 3:** The neutral palette of the shop is executed in concrete, reclaimed wood, and glass. Stenciled Navajo-style "rugs" highlight feature fixtures like this "drawing table" unit backed up with a floor-to-ceiling factory loft "window."

▶ **Figure 4:** In the denim area the hot-rolled steel wall units have rough, reclaimed wood as shelving. Note the back wall made of strips of old, recycled wood panels. All add to the "raw texture" of the denim presentation.

◀ **Figure 5:** Standing in front of the carefully merchandised denim wall is a fit guide—reminiscent of old cinema signage—along with samples of the various denim finishes for shoppers to touch and interact with. The industrial look is further enhanced by the table design.

◀ **Figure 6:** Muted reds and blues are used to create the faded flag fabric drapes hung to provide privacy in the unisex changing room. They, along with the pony skin covered Eames chairs, reinforce the Americana theme of this Wrangler outpost.

CASE STUDY 3.3

MAIDENFORM

SANTIAGO, CHILE

DESIGN: DROGUETT A&A, SANTIAGO, CHILE

DESIGN OBJECTIVE

Although Maidenform is a well known and respected brand in North America and in some European countries, until now it has only been sold in Chile through local distributors. During its more than 90-year history as a specialist in bras and body-shaping products of excellent quality and superior fit, Maidenform has built strong equity for its brand and established a platform for growth through a combination of innovative, first-to-market designs and creative advertising campaigns focused on increasing brand awareness with generations of women.

For its first stand-alone store in Santiago, the company called upon the Droguett A&A architectural design firm to create a retail space that would appeal to "high taste level, design-driven consumers seeking value; confidence seekers; early adopters; sensuality versus overtly sexy; neoclassical consumers—18- to 34-year-olds—seeking sensual style; and fashion-forward 40-year-olds—intimate enthusiasts." For many Chilean women, Maidenform was not a well known brand; therefore it had to make an effective first impression and it had to be a strong one.

DESIGN SOLUTION

Freddy Droguett says: "The first Chilean flagship needed to be an effective and recognizable small building that could transmit the brand values such as sophistication and sensuality—always seeking to enhance the brand image and create a strong emotional bond with Chilean consumers." An existing building was transformed with a second skin of lacquered plywood plaques that were perforated "with a sinuous grid of backlit squares" that reference lingerie lace. In one corner of the box-like structure there is a picture of a sensual model that suggests what is going on inside. This, Droguett explains, "gives the store a new regular and defined aspect that converts it into a black hermetic box that works as a giant sign for the illuminated logo but keeps the interior a delicate store with delicate merchandise. The contrast between the container (the hard box) and its delicate content is the major achievement of this project."

The interior of the store is dominated by the black and white palette complemented by the warmth of the bleached wood floors and delicate touches like the rugs, the gauzy curtains, and skin-flattering lamps. The fixtures are finished in black laminate and/or stainless steel and add the desired touch of sophistication to the simple interior design. All the fixtures are not only functional but flexible. Garments are highlighted and accentuated by the use of black wall panels to offset the soft-colored product display. Adding to the ambience is the lighting. Freddy Droguett says: "Lights are used in a theatrical way. Technical lighting is combined with decorative lamps that give a cozy and relaxed special mood and feel to the store. This mood helps the clients to feel as though they are at home and comfortable." Mannequins appear on low platforms and sitting on top of on-floor elements and they are supplemented by large colored graphics of models in Maidenform garments. He goes on:

> *Mannequins have always been a part of the retailer's visual strategy and here they are used in-store to provide more visual components that draw shoppers in and appeal to their desires. The direct visual experience of the mannequin is important so the customer can see how elastic fibers fit the woman's body. Body-shaping clothing needs to show how it fits.*

CONCLUSION

From the hot-pink logo "M" and the Maidenform name below, glowing against the inky black exterior of the retail outlet, to the simple yet sophisticated interior resplendent in warm light, the noted company has made an auspicious entry into a new market with its brand on full display. More Maidenform outlets are to be expected following this prototype design.

DESIGN CREDITS:

Design: Droguett A&A, Santiago, Chile
Freddy Droguett: Architect and Main Director
Marcelo Lopez: Architect/Partner and Director of Architecture
Cristian Luque and Tomas González: Retail Store Division Architects

Client: Maidenform
Victoria Izurieta: CEO
Rosa Maria Jensen: Marketing Manager
Silvio Cazatti: Operations Manager

Photography: Marcos Mendizábal / Droguett A&A Design Team

◀ **Figure 1:** The backlit, applied "skin" on the first Chilean Maidenform flagship stand-alone store suggests the lace trim of the intimate garments while the hot-pink illuminated logo "M" identifies the space. The models in the corner window show off the latest designs.

◀ **Figure 2:** The black and white color palette is complemented by the bleached oak floors and the recurring pink "M" logo. Large graphic blow-ups of ads add colorful accents to the space.

◤ Figure 3: The colored garments are set off by and step out from the black panels behind them. Individual dressing rooms are provided at the rear of the space and are identified by the logo "M."

◀ Figure 4: Seating is provided to encourage shoppers and their guests to stay a while in the comfortable and smart shop. Merchandise is artfully displayed on wall units as well as on free-standing floor displayers.

▲ Figure 5: Technical lighting is combined with fabric-covered drum shaded lamps that give a cozy, relaxed, and feminine feel to the shop. Stylized mannequins appear throughout to show how the garments look on the body. "Body-shaping clothing needs to show how it fits."

CASE STUDY 3.4

ALLEN SOLLY

BANGALORE, INDIA

DESIGN: DALZIEL + POW, LONDON, UK

DESIGN OBJECTIVE

The Allens of Nottinghamshire in England opened their warehouse in 1744 and by 1811 were exporting British items to the United States. In 1831 the Allen family was joined in marriage to the Sollys of Kent and the Solly capital added to the Allen craftsmanship combined to become the Allen, Solly Inc. brand. By 1850 the company was exporting goods to over 50 countries. Now we skip ahead a century and more to 1993 when the Allen Solly brand appeared in retail stores in India. The brand was taken over by Madura Garments (now Madura Fashion & Lifestyle) who, according to the Allen Solly website, "realized that there was a burgeoning market in catering to professionals that they had not yet explored. These were the professionals unhappy with the status quo and looking for something that was quite out of the ordinary. Allen Solly was reborn as an answer to their quest. Friday Dressing was introduced to the Indian corporate wardrobe. Overnight, Allen Solly became famous for Friday Dressing and the brand models became role models." In 2001 the Aditya Birla Group obtained the world rights to the brand and a new chapter began for the Allen Solly brand. A year later, Women's Work clothing was introduced. According to the Allen Solly website, "Convention is not a word that exists in the brand's vocabulary and from the beginning the brand not only broke the rules of formal workplace dressing, but also rewrote them. The dull world of business dressing with its grays and whites was shaken up by Allen Solly, which unapologetically added vibrant dashes of color to its formal wear line."

Keith Ware, Group Development Director of Dalziel + Pow, the London-based design consultancy, explains: "Friday Dressing set the benchmark for dressing young professionals in the early '90s and the Allen Solly brand became synonymous with India's development by catering for the needs of the emerging professional middle class. Our brief, as designers, was to refine the brand's position within the Indian market, with casual style at its core, and to excite the customer with a contemporary Indian environment whilst adding a 'quintessentially British' twist. We refreshed the logo and designed the new store environment and communications."

DESIGN SOLUTION

Ware explains:

> *Initially we defined the Allen Solly target customer—their influences, references, and aspirations—to create a full perspective of their target audience. From this platform we created an environment and communications that were able to deliver the essence of the brand's personality, capturing a mix of heritage styling within a contemporary space and creating a strong identity for the store. We put the brand's core values of freedom and effortless style at the forefront of the design. The concept comprises a backdrop of painted brickwork, utilitarian loft-style merchandising, and traditional herringbone wood flooring which brings an element of domesticity to the architecture. The graphic approach is eclectic, and the store has an equally diverse collection of finishes and treatments. Found objects such as colored decorative lamps and Allen Solly's bespoke custom tartan fabric are layered into the scheme—adding a rich splash of color. The successful blend of these elements has revitalized the brand and the store environment, making it relevant to today's Allen Solly customer.*

Starting at the all-glass, two-story façade and continuing throughout the space in various forms and graphic treatments is the stag's head logo that has become the new corporate identity of the Allen Solly brand. It is the symbol of the brand which started in Nottinghamshire in the UK over 270 years ago and is its heritage. A giant white antlered head appears centered over the store name on the façade and the logo/brand name appears inside on a painted brick wall. Miniature heads are lined up in a pattern on a focal wall or appear individually as reminders that this is Allen Solly territory.

CONCLUSION

While the Allen Solly approach to business wear has been successful, it has also spawned many imitators—but, as the Aditya Birla Group asserts on the Allen Solly website, "The unconventional, yet unmistakable Allen Solly Man never lost his place in the spotlight. Today it is one of India's most popular and easily recognized brands in the branded premium apparel segment. Consumers understand it as a vibrant and upbeat work-wear brand." Currently there are over 160 Allen Solly stores located in 76 cities in India.

DESIGN CREDITS:

Design:	Dalziel + Pow, London, UK David Dalziel: Creative Director Keith Ware: Group Development Director
Client:	Allen Solly
Photography:	Marmit Singh / Courtesy of Dalziel + Pow

▶ **Figure 1:**
The stag's head, the new corporate logo for Allen Solly, dominates the all-glass, two-story façade of the store. It appears over the brand name on the window and reappears throughout the interior design.

▼ **Figure 2:** The shop caters to professional men and women and is popular with those who prefer "vibrant dashes of color in their formal wear." "Convention does not exist in the brand's vocabulary."

◀ **Figure 3:**
The stag's head logo appears on the white brick wall. The store design captures "a mix of heritage styling within a contemporary space and creates a strong identity for the store."

◀ **Figure 4:**
The concept includes "a backdrop of painted brickwork, utilitarian loft-style merchandising, and traditional herringbone wood flooring, which brings an element of domesticity to the architecture."

◀ **Figure 5:** Women's wear is a relatively new addition to the Allen Solly 200-plus years of heritage and has an area all of its own in the store.

◣ **Figure 6:** In the women's wear department there is lots of color in the product display. The painted white brick, herringbone floors, and Allen Solly's custom tartan fabric are added to the scheme, "adding a rich splash of color." Altogether, the blend makes the store relevant to today's Allen Solly customer.

CASE STUDY 3.5

CARLO PAZOLINI

SOHO, NEW YORK CITY, USA

DESIGN: GIORGIO BORRUSO DESIGN, MARINA DEL REY, CALIFORNIA, USA

DESIGN OBJECTIVE

Giorgio Borruso is one of the most respected of today's retail store architects/designers and has worked with fashion brands for over two decades. His retail store designs for Carlo Pazolini have won numerous design awards and his particular approach to designing spaces is captured in the following quote: "We were looking to create an environment that reflects the best aspiration of the brand—a combination of profound understanding of the product and knowledge of ancient materials with the most advanced techniques. Spaces are not just interiors but have energy and movement. Spaces have a role in the city that incorporate and respect the history of the surroundings that express their confidence and originality." The Italian look and feel of the brand would have to find a way to agreeably and eloquently speak its design language in a typically SoHo NYC setting.

DESIGN SOLUTION

Signature elements that have appeared in previous Carlo Pazolini stores such as long, sinuous lines, soft and voluptuous curves, and petal-like shelves in green, orange, and gray—all contained in a mostly white space accented in black—appear here. These signature design elements stamp the brand name on the space, although each space is especially created to suit its location. We will let Giorgio Borruso explain:

> *Carlo Pazolini SoHo flagship in New York City is a 4000 sq. ft retailer of Italian women's and men's shoes and accessories located in the long, narrow ground floor of what was originally a warehouse typical of the Cast Iron Historic District. Fluctuating between only 10 feet wide at the entrance to 20 feet wide at the rear of the sales floor, and measuring 130 feet long, the spatial elements were unique but also dramatic, and this is something we sought to reinforce. Issues of spatial compression and release in relation to program and movement began to form the overarching architectural theme. The ceiling and women's wall take on a fluid but ripped geometry which creates a procession from the entry to the rear of the store. After entering*

from the street, where the scale is urban and vertically extreme, the space immediately contracts down to 9 feet by 9 feet and then opens up again to 12 feet by 15 feet near the cash/wrap desk. This extreme modification of scale serves as a transition between the street and the store and acts as a "cleansing" experience that prepares visitors for the space beyond.

The women's wall is populated by a series of colorful molded resin and natural wool felt display units. The inspiration for the cellular forms, which are also used as seating, comes from the way the human foot's network of bones and tendons physically adapt to the specificities of footwear. To create a simultaneous sense of shaping and being shaped, we used the form of an infant's foot as an iconic cell in a "swarm" (insect swarms, bird flocks) network of women's display shelving and seating that form an ambiguously stippled spatial condition in which the object and the space containing it become less rigidly explicit. These cellular display units are complemented with long white horizontal shelves that suggest a streaked or ripped movement along the wall surface in perspective, tying the wall to the ceiling geometries.

The opposing men's wall also finds its root in "swarm" logic but manifests itself in a different way. MDF shelves are finished in a dark brown stain with white lacquer edges, and fade between open areas for mirror viewing and dense areas for display. The shelves appear to float on the long full-height mirror wall, which in turn aids in opening up the space in an ephemeral way without breaking down the manipulations of scale by the women's wall and ceiling forms. Between these two opposing "swarms," the ceiling undulates and twists as if strange behemoths were silently passing overhead, acting as a spatial stitch between the men's and women's wall, but also as an agitator that manipulates the scale and density of the overall architectural envelope. It can be thought of as the fluid dynamic manifestation of the water or air currents that move through the space.

CONCLUSION

This design was immediately followed by other award-winning solutions in London and Venice. The success of the Carlo Pazolini brand combined with the design language that Giorgio Borruso adapts to the various locations remain, and continue to be, a winning combination no matter where the stores may be.

DESIGN CREDITS:

Design:	Giorgio Borruso Design, Marina del Rey, California, USA Giorgio Borruso: Architect/Designer
Client:	Carlo Pazolini
Photography:	Courtesy of Magda Biernat

◀ **Figure 1:** Behind the traditional, century-old, cast-iron façade is the new and exciting Carlo Pazolini shoe store. The modern, free-flowing architecture and the splashes of color are visible through the wide window.

◀ **Figure 2:** Long, sinuous lines, soft curves, petal-like shelves in signature green, gray, and orange, and slivers of mirror are all recognizable elements seen in other Carlo Pazolini stores around the world

◀ **Figure 3:** The mirrored wall, here on the left, "aids in opening up the space in an ephemeral way without breaking down the manipulations of scale by the women's wall and ceiling forms."

◀ **Figure 4:** "The ceiling undulates and twists as if strange behemoths were silently passing overhead, acting as a spatial stitch between the men's and women's wall." The general lighting fills the spaces between the floating ceiling panels.

▲ **Figure 5:** Soft, curving shelves—white on white—make their way to the cash/wrap desk, which seems to evolve from the flowing forms. The lines resemble "the fluid dynamic manifestation of water or air currents that move through space."

◀ **Figure 6:** Cutting through the stark white space—like the prow of a ship—is the graceful cash/wrap desk. The Carlo Pazolini logo appears discreetly on the wall behind it to mark the area.

CASE STUDY 3.6

JOE FRESH

FIFTH AVENUE, NEW YORK CITY, USA

DESIGN: BURDIFILEK, TORONTO, CANADA

DESIGN OBJECTIVE

Having worked with the Joe Fresh brand since its inception seven years ago and designing its stores in Canada, Diego Burdi and Paul Filek of the Burdifilek design firm in Toronto were ready and able to take on the new assignment. The challenge was to create the brand identity of this stylish and affordable line of clothing and accessories for men, women, and children in New York City. The Joe Fresh company had taken over the 17,000 sq. ft landmark modernist building on the corner of Fifth Avenue and 43rd Street in Manhattan and asked the Burdifilek team to create an interior that would complement the Joe Fresh brand. Diego Burdi, the Creative Partner of the design firm, described the brand as "young, modern, and with a hip feel" and the aim was to create "a clean and spacious interior with various textures to frame the Joe Fresh offer."

DESIGN SOLUTION

Diego Burdi explains: "The store interior embraces its architectural bones and opens to its surroundings. We kept the store open to the spectacular views of New York City which we regard as moving wallpaper. The store is airy, colorful, urban, and ever-changing—underscoring what Joe Fresh is about." The building is wrapped with 27 ft high glass windows that showcase the interior and the floating white terrazzo mezzanine. To protect the historic features of the building, no fixtures were drilled into the walls, floors, or ceilings. To complement the essential lightness of the building, free-floating sculptural merchandising systems were designed and, according to Burdi, "These custom-designed wardrobes can be easily arranged and reconfigured into vignettes to separate collections and to break down the space as desired." Each vignette tells a different color story and the all-white ambience was designed to enhance the Joe Fresh color presentations. The wardrobes are made of white, powder-coated metal with sandblasted Lexan panels to transmit light. "Incorporating seamless monitors, mirrors, or backlit billboards, they are radiant and dynamic, and along with a select number of glowing light boxes in Joe Fresh's signature orange and video screens displaying contemporary art videos or runway shows, they contribute to the liveliness of the store and allow the merchandise to glow," adds

Diego Burdi. Just as Joe Fresh pays attention to detail and proportion in its fashions, the designers paid careful attention in designing the fixtures and furniture used in the store. Powder-coated aluminum "Parsons" tables and benches are used for on-floor displayers along with white polycarbonate merchandising cubes. The cubes are poured from wood molds so they have the texture of wood grains and the appearance of porcelain. The signature orange color brings the Joe Fresh brand into play throughout the store. It appears in the large changing rooms on the seating cubes that are wrapped in orange neoprene and as an accent throughout the store. At night the store glows in orange and serves to attract shoppers on the street.

The space resembles a gallery-like experience in reflecting the historical importance of the building with its architectural finishes and sculptural fixtures. Adding a unique look to the store and serving as a separator and setting is the 70 ft long gilded metal screen designed by the modernist sculptor/furniture designer Harry Bertoia. Bertoia also designed the hanging "cloud" mobile that adds an artistic and whimsical touch to it all. According to Burdi, they "provide a creative point of reference for shoppers as visual touch points within the space."

CONCLUSION

"Joe Fresh is proudly Canadian, and reflecting that, our design is confident yet understated. If you look closely, you'll find subtle but sophisticated nuances that create interest and distinguish the Joe Fresh aesthetic" and brand, adds Burdi. Other than the use of the signature orange color, the brand is introduced in "subtle but sophisticated nuances."

Paul Filek, the Managing Partner at Burdifilek, adds his comment on the importance of designing for brand perception:

> *The retailer must engage their customers in a compelling manner to make the brand stand out from the rest. Working with Joe Fresh to strengthen their presence required a design that visually reinforced the brand's identity. Like their product, a sophisticated, modern store was designed to add value to the offering and reflect its fashion-forward appeal. Having attracted both the mass market target group as well as the well-heeled Fifth Avenue shopper has earned this retailer recognition in the world of fashion.*

DESIGN CREDITS:

Design:	Burdifilek, Toronto, Canada
	Diego Burdi: Creative Partner
	Paul Filek: Managing Partner
	Jeremy Mendonica: Senior Designer
	Jacky Kwong: Designer
	Daniel Mei, Edwin Reyes, Anna Nomerovsky, Anthony Tey, Daniela Cerchie: CADD
	Tom Yip: Project Manager
Client:	Joe Fresh
Photography:	Ben Rahn at A-Frame Studio

◀ **Figure 1:** The almost all glass Joe Fresh store glows with the brand's signature orange color and attracts shoppers on Fifth Avenue. Its open and airy design is readily viewed from outside.

▶ **Figure 2:** Tall, floor-to-ceiling windows combined with an illuminated ceiling and all-white flexible and moveable fixtures create the desired setting for the urban, hip line of clothing shown here.

◀ Figure 3: Orange IS the Joe Fresh color and it appears throughout the otherwise white interior. Here, it is vibrant at the entrance and the escalator that leads to the terrazzo mezzanine.

◀ Figure 4: This shows the approach to the upper level and the 70 ft gilded metal sculptural wall that serves as a divider and setting for the white abstract mannequins in Joe Fresh outfits.

◀ **Figure 5:** The color story predominates in the merchandise presentation, and the moveable fixtures make it possible to quickly reconfigure the selling spaces.

▶ **Figure 6:** The merchandising cabinets are of white powder-coated metal with sandblasted Lexan panels to transmit light; they can be reconfigured into separate color-coordinated vignettes. A transparent rail surrounds the mezzanine level, adding to the floating feeling.

▶ **Figure 7:** The cloud mobile, floating over the cluster of mannequins, was also created by Bertoia. It is visible from the street as well.

◀ **Figure 8:** A detail of the metal screen designed by Harry Bertoia. No fixtures were drilled, nailed, or screwed into the landmark building interior; all fixtures are free standing.

CASE STUDY 3.7

PUMA OSAKA

OSAKA, JAPAN

DESIGN: PLAJER & FRANZ STUDIO, BERLIN, GERMANY

DESIGN OBJECTIVE

The architects and designers at plajer & franz studio, a design firm in Berlin, working closely with Ales Kernjak, the head of global store concepts for PUMA, evolved the new PUMA store in Osaka, Japan. The premium store is breathtaking in size and scope, filling the over 6000 sq. ft space on two levels with the PUMA collections. According to Patricia Senft, who served as project manager along with Anne-Kathrin Hahn, "Both the exterior and interior architecture of the space have been PUMA-rized and speak a homogenous language that unifies the company's philosophy, an intelligent yet simple retail design, and the joyful and witty spirit of the sport-lifestyle brand." The design not only had to present the variety of PUMA products and their suitable activities but also had to invite the youthful Japanese shoppers into this world of PUMA with enough nods to Japanese art and culture to make the store a comfortable fit for the location.

DESIGN SOLUTION

The exterior façade consists of red meshed metal baffles that allow daylight in during the daytime and glow from the internal lighting at night. Patricia Senft explains the challenge the designers faced:

> *The interior architecture included the design and development of the individual concepts for different PUMA product categories such as "performance," "sport-lifestyle," and "black label" as well as a special destination area for the "PUMA factory." To unite these different concepts with differentiated visual languages and still develop a homogeneous store design that brings "joy" back to life and includes some local reference was a particularly demanding task. In addition, the concepts for the "performance" area and "black label" were new concept developments. By keeping the overall design simple and flexible and by authentically reflecting the image of the brand the unity could be accomplished.*

Acknowledging the store's location in Japan and catering to the Japanese market, the designers at plajer & franz studio have kept the overall design quite simple with an occasional reference to Japanese art and culture. There are origami-like seating elements in the sport-lifestyle area and the use of materials like wood and concrete. Werner Franz, CEO and founder of the design firm, explains: "To add a 'local influence' is a way for the brand to communicate with the customer on a very personal level. By including local aspects in the retail design the brand gives the consumers a feeling that it respects the location, its particularities, and especially that it values the demands and desires of the local customers."

He continues: "Every product area speaks a different visual language and is clearly distinct from each other. For the Performance area on the upper floor we used rather technical materials such as stainless steel or perforated metal in silver gray to highlight the 'performance' message. The Black Label area, on the other hand, is characterized by a very light and flexible design. Here, we used materials such as black steel and plywood panels and combined them with reused gym flooring elements. The idea was to give this area a visible sports heritage."

The interior is dominated by the sweeping staircase that connects the two retail levels and by the signature red wall with the leaping puma logo. "It is the eye catcher, making a strong brand statement, and serves as the key ingredient to converging the PUMA brand—performance and sport-lifestyle—with functional design. Emulating an amphitheater, the staircase boasts the striking red brand wall in the background and is the place where the product and the brand are celebrated at full blast. It is like a stage for the great performance of the product—notably footwear." It draws attention not only to its design but, above all, to the Footwear Tribune at the foot of it. In this PUMA brandstore, "the staircase together with the brandwall can be seen somehow as the heart of the place," adds Patricia Senft. "This 'stage' continues as a footwear catwalk stretching across the entire ground level where the Sport-Lifestyle and Black Label product lines are on display." The architectural design of this level—the entire store in fact—"aims at strengthening the brand image and enhancing the display of PUMA's collections, while celebrating footwear as the core of the brand." Throughout there are accents of the signature PUMA red color brightening up the neutral color palette of the floor and adding "joy" to the space.

Shoppers make it up the grand sweep of the stunning staircase and its multi-cube textured red wall to arrive at the upper level, which is dedicated to the Performance area. As Werner Franz explains, "The nature of performance is visible and perceptible throughout. The brandstore is more than just a shopping place. It is a social and cultural meeting point—a space for events and happenings of various kinds." The open rooftop serves as the ideal space for events and happenings of various kinds. Sport screenings, tournaments, concerts, and similar events are organized to bring the like-minded community together.

CONCLUSION

"Shopping at the new premium store is above all an experience and, in line with PUMA's philosophy, an active interaction with the brand. Whether creating their own customized sneakers at the PUMA Factory, engaging with PUMA's sustainable actions summarized in the Sustainability Journey, or enjoying the online experience via iPads, clients shall be surprised, entertained, and given opportunities to identify with the brand." Werner Franz concludes: "We have already worked with PUMA for a while ... redesigning stores literally around the world. The collaboration goes on and we have to expect new and surprising retail concepts as PUMA is 'redirecting' itself to a more 'performance' oriented brand."

DESIGN CREDITS:

Design:	plajer & franz studio, Berlin, Germany Werner Franz: CEO and Founder Patricia Senft and Anne-Kathrin Hahn: Project Managers Under the direction of Ales Kernjak, PUMA AG
Client:	PUMA Ales Kernjak: Head of Global Store Concepts
Local Architect:	MD Associates, Tokyo, Japan
Building Contractor:	Konoike Konstruction, Japan
Graphic Works and Visual Communications:	Studio 38, Berlin, Germany
Rotating Shoes:	Brandon AR, Goteborg, Sweden
Shopfitting:	Max Brilliant in-store Supply, Shanghai and Nomura Co. Ltd, Tokyo
Photography:	diephotodesigner.de

▶ **Figure 1:** Signature PUMA red meshed metal baffles cover the façade of the PUMA store in Osaka. Through the openings shoppers can see some of the interior display.

▼ **Figure 2:** Natural wood and concrete are the major materials in creating a simple and functional Japanese-inspired interior. The ceiling is blacked out and metal pipe merchandising cubes hang down from above.

◀ **Figure 3:** The focal element in the store is the sweeping staircase, the signature red wall with white puma, and a red dot stage to start the action. Footwear is featured in tiers on the right wall as part of the Footwear Tribune.

◀ **Figure 4:** Highlighting a display area is a Japanese-inspired treatment of PUMA-red paper lanterns. The Black Label and Sport-Lifestyle collections are featured at ground level along with PUMA footwear.

▶ **Figure 5:** A view of the upper retail level and the dressed abstract mannequins that appear throughout the space, highlighting the different fashion collections.

◀ **Figure 6:** Stainless steel and gray painted perforated metal add to the look here, as do the flexible tables with convertible covers.

◀ **Figure 7:** The entire upper floor is dedicated to performance wear. On the right is a perforated metal wall and a collection of performance footwear. Numbered cubes with accents of PUMA red serve as seating. Giant graphics and dressed mannequins add other shots of color.

◀ **Figure 8:** The store was designed to also serve as a meeting place as well as an occasional performance area and for special events. Clients "are surprised, entertained and given opportunities to identify with the brand."

CASE STUDY 3.8

WAWA

CENTRAL FLORIDA

DESIGN: CBX, NEW YORK, USA

DESIGN OBJECTIVE

With over 600 Wawa convenience stores located in Pennsylvania, Maryland, New Jersey, Delaware, and Virginia, the odd name is certainly familiar to travelers in the mid-Atlantic states. However, what the Wawa brand stands for was not so well known in central Florida, where the company decided to make their entry into the field of fast food/fast service. Joseph Bona, the President of Branded Environments at the NYC-based CBX design firm and a long-time designer of "c" (for Convenience) stores, took up the challenge offered by Wawa's President and CEO, Chris Gheysens, to design the new look for the Florida rollout. Gheysens says: "We felt we needed a fresh design driven by the psychology of the Florida customer."

DESIGN SOLUTION

Joe Bona explains:

> *With its signature coffee bar, open kitchen, fresh-baked goods, and other distinguishing characteristics, Wawa needed to make sure Floridians understood this new entry was a cut above other convenience stores. People tend to think of any building with gas pumps as a run-of-the-mill convenience store, but we were intent on making sure Wawa's brand did not fall victim to this "gas penalty." The design needed to reflect Wawa's "fresh and inviting" brand essence and be relevant to the Florida customer.*

In recognition of the c-store's new Florida location, the façade is finished in tropical pastel colors and the clapboard siding and pitched roofs along with the front porch acknowledge the architecture of the area. But still familiar to travelers who know Wawa from the mid-Atlantic states are the "winged" canopies over the gas pumps and the Canada goose logo. The new interior design "reflects the language and style associated with Floridian vernacular architecture." There is an open and spacious feel to the interior with its high ceilings and lots of natural light. The red-tiled wall highlights the all-important center island kitchen where it is possible to order any specialty drink or sandwich "made to your order" by means of a unique touch-screen system. There are a series of screens conveniently located at the kitchen/specialty drink areas' counters. In addition, digital signage is used to present the foods and beverages in a fun and contemporary manner. A warm taupe tiled wall accentuates the counter adjoined by the coffee and beverage sections. Overhead, red drum shaded lighting fixtures "create a sense of space" over the coffee area and the beverage coolers. Throughout, "fresh" decorating cues appear as in the use of natural materials, the tall glass windows, and the hospitably warm color palette.

CONCLUSION

As Chris Gheysens of Wawa explains, "The new store design has really informed people who didn't previously know Wawa and what the brand stands for: it stands for 'fresh'—great quality foods and beverages—and convenience. When you walk into the store, you see people making food as well as digital signs romancing the offer. There's no mistaking that we are in the fresh food and fresh beverage business." Joe Bona of CBX adds: "We're delighted that customers and peers are giving Wawa's design rave reviews." Among those "rave reviews," the store was named *Convenience Store News* magazine's "Innovator of the Year," with special acknowledgment for its innovative use of the social media, a mobile app initiative, and Wawa's continued focus on the consumer.

DESIGN CREDITS:

Design:	CBX, New York, USA
	Joseph Bona: President of Branded Environments, CBX NY
Client:	Wawa
	Chris Gheysens: President and CEO
Photographer:	Blandon Belushin

▶ **Figure 1:** Pitched roof, pastel colors, and a welcoming front porch set the Floridian look for this mid-Atlantic states convenience store operation's move into the Florida market. The familiar flying canopy over the gas pumps is seen on the right.

◀ **Figure 2:** High ceilings and warm, friendly colors accented in red make the interior seem spacious. Daylight streams in through the many windows, adding to the feeling of openness.

Wawa Single Cups
Step 2
Shop & Pay

◤ **Figure 3:** The open, centrally located kitchen where sandwiches and beverages are made to order is highlighted by the clever digital menu boards and monitor screens overhead. It is backed up by the signature red tiled wall.

◀ **Figure 4:** The beverage area is located near the taupe-colored tile wall—beyond the central kitchen—and accented by the red drum lampshades suspended over the area. Light-colored wood appears throughout.

▲ **Figure 5:** The ebony-faced refrigerated cases line up along a perimeter wall near the snack foods and under a line of red drum lampshades. Floridians have been charmed by the "fast food gourmet" offerings in this Florida-friendly setting.

CASE STUDY 3.9

WHOLE FOODS

MACK AVENUE, DETROIT, MICHIGAN, USA

DESIGN: JGA, SOUTHFIELD, MICHIGAN, USA

DESIGN OBJECTIVE

The design objective presented to the design team at JGA of Southfield, Michigan was "to create a more 'city right' concept using local signature icons." At the same time, this new Whole Foods 25,500 sq. ft supermarket, located in Detroit, Michigan, also had to live up to the brand's belief in being "responsible commerce" when it comes to the locality, nature, and the general environment. The press release offered by the JGA design firm states: "The Detroit city location lives up to these principles not only in what it purveys, or through the associates in the store, but as well with its environment and building in which it conducts its business. Design partners, local artists, and fabricators joined with the Whole Foods team to create a fusion of food and place through reclaiming, repurposing, and even reimagining pieces of Detroit's past into an expression of Detroit's future."

DESIGN SOLUTION

The store's appeal is focused on the young urban residents, the neighborhood dwellers, and the working population around the store who see it as a place to enjoy a healthy lunch, stop off for the evening's dinner, or do the weekly shopping for healthy, natural, and tasty foods. According to Ken Nisch, Chairman and Project Principal of JGA, "The character of the store creates an instant connection with the shopper in the neighborhood; a neighborhood that represents the past, present and future of urban Detroit and its eclectic, colorful and welcoming message to those looking to contribute to the future of the city."

In addition to the traditional supermarket food areas like cheeses and dairy products, the bakery, and assorted prepared specialty foods—both local and international—there is an expanded café.

The brand's commitment to the environment and to sustainability is evident in the designers' use of reclaimed and repurposed objects for the building materials as well as the decorative elements. The inspiration for the store's layout is the unique street grid that is particular to Detroit and its French roots, which features radial streets, avenues, and squares.

These elements appear in the background graphics, directional signage and cornice treatments. The Cooking area features a design constructed of sculpted squares of repurposed broomstick material that has been laser cut into a dimensional graphic. Shoppers are reminded that Detroit is the "Motor City" by the Bakery heading treatment that consists of a series of metal conduits bent to simulate auto tail pipes. For identifying the Specialty Foods location, a collage of reclaimed signs—street, business, all sorts—have been rescued from scrap piles "to become a colorful, eclectic and locally relevant diary of the areas past." And the city's Motown musical heritage is evident in the use of the vinyl LP records that highlight the checkout counters. Since graffiti is part of almost every urban environment, the corrugated metal background of the Cheese department is covered with that artistic expression. Remnants of the city's industrial heritage, like reclaimed auto hoods and furniture, are used creatively and repurposed as tables, chairs, and serving units. The front entry into the store is faced with reclaimed thin bricks and the factory windows that were used were rescued from an industrial factory and thus saved from landfill.

Combining Detroit's history, popular culture, and its ongoing reinvention is the Heritage Timeline that appears over the refrigerator cases along the perimeter wall in the store.

CONCLUSION

Ken Nisch summed it up this way:

> *Whole Foods has successfully broadened the consumer's appetite for health products through a unique and global cuisine and socially responsible consumption. While it has broadened the consumer's point of view, it as well has been highly successful in localizing the consumer's interest and aspiration for food that is seasonal, regional, and local. Its store environment is mirroring that same purpose of being creatively provocative, but is in tune locally, be it from a content, materiality and as well, through the use of local resources, artists, and fabricators. Whole Foods Detroit takes us to an even higher level, leveraging Detroit's reputation as a place where things are made by people and by using ordinary objects and materials, but bringing them together in extraordinary ways.*

DESIGN CREDITS:

Design:	JGA, Southfield, Michigan, USA Ken Nisch: Chairman and Project Principal Michael Curtis: Creative Director
Client:	Whole Foods Christine Sturch: Midwest Senior Interior Design and Branding Coordinator Stacey Landino: Midwest Associate Design and Signage Coordinator
General Contractor:	Sachse Construction, Birmingham, Michigan, USA
Lighting Designer:	Western Extralite, Kansas City, Missouri, USA
Graphics and Signage:	Design Fabrications, Madison Heights, Michigan, USA Tony Camilletti
Salvage Graphic Element Consultant:	Marisa Gaggino, Heritage Co. II / Royal Oak, Michigan, USA
Millwork:	Doors & Drawers, Dexter, Michigan, USA Chuck Manitz Capital Wood Products, St. Paul, Minnesota, USA Jim Juris
Photography:	Nicole Reedy, WFM Midwest Regional Art Director Jenn Hulbert, WFM Chicago Metro Marketing Team Leader

◀ **Figure 1:** Right up front, Whole Foods announces its community ties. The background is a graphic rendering on the streets, avenues, and plazas that are unique to the layout of Detroit.

▶ Figure 2:
Sustainability is part of the Whole Foods brand and the store features many reclaimed and repurposed elements, like the factory windows from a destroyed plant that now appear over the Food area.

▶ Figure 3:
Sammies Pizza is defined by the many and varied reclaimed signs that are fashioned into an exciting collage over the counter.

◀ Figure 8: Many think of Detroit as "Motown" and know of its musical tradition. Motown records serve as checkout lane markers. Note the Community Support Day sign—another indication of Whole Foods being part of the community.

CASE STUDY 3.10

JANSPORT

MALL OF GEORGIA, BUFORD, GEORGIA, USA

DESIGN: TWENTY FOUR 7, PORTLAND, OREGON, USA

DESIGN OBJECTIVE

JanSport, the original backpack company, has been equipping people globally with quality backpacks, travel gear, and collegiate apparel since its inception in 1967. In an effort to bring the product to the public, and not in an enclosed retail space, JanSport challenged the design firm Twenty Four 7, based in Portland, Oregon, to design a kiosk that would display the brand's merchandise effectively.

Mimi Lettunich, Executive Director at Twenty Four 7 explains:

> *We were asked to design a kiosk concept that breaks the mold and represents the brand in a manner consistent with JanSport's full-size retail environment. The design had to be flexible and maintain the brand presence when open or folded and closed at night. In addition, it had to maximize sales and flexibility in a small footprint to accommodate the range of JanSport products.*

DESIGN SOLUTION

What Twenty Four 7 designed, engineered, and built was a cube that could transform into an open and engaging retail environment with visual merchandising and product messaging. The fixtures are easy to shop on the interior but secured on the exterior for display. The wood-toned unit, sustainably designed using reclaimed lumber and powder-coated metals, meets all of the brand's design standards while maximizing JanSport's message to its target market. It has a rugged, out-of-doors feel to it. In many ways, the finished unit appeals to that market which Ms. Lettunich describes as "youthful, energetic, urban, and fun-loving." She continues: "JanSport is known for quality with an approachable brand personality for those who use the product in urban environments or the great outdoors. That spirit is reflected in the kiosk design with a balance of innovation, functionality, contemporary lines, and the mix of raw, refined, and reclaimed materials."

The fact that the kiosk unfolds and closes into a protected cube at night makes it almost

▶ **Figure 3:** Backlit graphics on the outer wall of the fixture adds to the kiosk's attraction and also makes a strong brand appeal to the target market.

▶ **Figure 4:** The merchandise on the outer wall is tethered so that it cannot be removed. It is purely for display.

▲ Figure 5: At night the entire shop folds up and stores into a compact unit as seen here. The illuminated brand sign, the graphic corner, and the secured backpacks remain on view.

CASE STUDY 3.11

ADIDAS

SPACE NINETY 8, WILLIAMSBURG, BROOKLYN, NEW YORK, USA

DESIGN: ROUNDHOUSE, PORTLAND, OREGON, USA

DESIGN OBJECTIVE

In 1972, at the Olympic Games in Munich, adidas presented a new logo that commemorated a commitment to athletic ideals: the Trefoil. Over the years, what first recognized sports performance grew to stand for something more. The Trefoil went beyond sport and started appearing on celebrities, influencers, and tastemakers. Today, the adidas Originals collection represents a legacy of sport, lifestyle, and the street. Identifying retailers with common consumers was one thing; creating lasting partnerships was another. A relationship between adidas Originals and Urban Outfitters began, and in 2014, it rose to the next level. To mark the event, something new was called for.

Roundhouse, a design firm based in Portland, Oregon, was called upon to help design a pop-up shop inside two Urban Outfitters retail spaces. Joe Sundby, Creative Director of Roundhouse, explains: "They asked for our help in creating an adidas brand experience within the space—one that would feature adidas blue and Original products. In each of the spaces, adidas wanted a localized and unique concept rooted in art and music that would be both authentic to the brand and to the Urban Outfitter consumer. The two spaces could hardly be farther apart geographically and from design standpoints. Space Ninety 8 in Williamsburg was located in a building basement pre-loaded with legitimate NYC street style, while Space 15 Twenty in LA was all windows, sunlight and living the California good life." A strong first impression was called for.

DESIGN SOLUTION

Sundby continues:

> *With years of adidas projects and campaigns in our portfolio, we had become quite familiar with the adidas Originals brand story. Authentic and unposed lifestyle moments, artist incorporation, pops of color, authentic street settings, inclusive and affirmative messaging—all came into play in the print, retail, digital, experiential, and social activations we created to convey what it means to be a true adidas Original. What*

Roundhouse concepted and brought to reality in the Urban Outfitter locations tapped into this relationship and continued the adidas Originals story. Our team factored in the unique personalities of adidas and Urban Outfitters, the even more unique personalities within the audiences shared by them, the works of renowned street artist Jason Woodside, designs, sketches, and shopping inventories to assemble a look that would transform the spaces into suites of shopping and celebration.

To create an environment where UO [Urban Outfitters] consumers could envision their own personality and fashion senses coming to life, the space was arranged to allow a large degree of engagement to be sparked by Jason Woodside's art as well as fashions and activation featured within the space. The overall aesthetic presented an artistic balance between adidas Originals, Williamsburg, and UO styles to create an adidas brand experience that still feels unique, on trend, and accommodating to our consumers' eclectic sense of style.

Reclaimed materials struck a balance with adidas Originals whites and blues to create a visually clean palette, allowing the works and installations of artist Jason Woodside to really pop. In graphic wraps, prints, overlays, and decals, Jason's patterned art was applied throughout the space on different visual planes and across unique textures. This infusion served to create almost instinctual pathways, facilitating traffic flow and building a common theme across the various furnishing, decorative, and aesthetic styles coexisting in the space. Joe Sundby explains: "Jason's artwork was also integrated with the flow of the staircase, adding a dynamic organic element to a functional environment and hinting at the incredible space below. Lightweight, printed graphic applications spread across the roof from the base of the staircase and lead to the focal point of the shop—the footwear wall."

A large trefoil, positioned over an extruded base, provides footwear display solutions and informs the shoe shelves extending from it. The extruded edges of the individual trefoil leaves provide a 'cubby' space to showcase the hero shoes of the featured collection, and Jason's art provides the background for an interesting presentation. The extruded base of the trefoil also showcases Jason's art and adds to the dimensionality of the display. Furthermore, Sundy explains, "To create an adidas experience that merged with the aesthetic of the space, toolkit imagery as well as US and global brand photography will be printed on oversized canvas frames. Minimal industrial-style fixtures lent a sense of lightness to the basement and presented a feminine aesthetic to the modern space."

As an oasis within Urban Outfitters, the lounge offers the consumer an opportunity to be immersed in a more extensive experience, with props and fixtures that evoke the hip hop/NYC/basketball scene and localize the global brand influences. The geometric qualities of select furniture pieces subtly complement Jason's work, and their placement maintains the premium, open aesthetic established by the space.

The physical differences between the NYC and LA retail spaces presented challenges. Moving from below ground in Williamsburg to a space featuring large windowed walls and high ceilings meant recalibrating fixture and furniture placements, reinterpreting Jason Woodside's artistic contributions, reselecting adidas Originals visual assets, and reorienting the focal footwear wall, among other just as crucial things. The airy and uncluttered environment was kept intact as Roundhouse introduced lightweight, geometric fixtures and accessories as well as hanging banners to showcase lookbook-style imagery, framing materials, and styles similar to those displayed in NYC in a whole new light.

CONCLUSION

The NYC and LA shops lived for six weeks with ongoing activations throughout, including launch events featuring opportunities to win vinyl records curated by Elijah Wood and Zach Cowie. Attendees could also bid on Jason Woodside-customized Stan Smiths, with proceeds benefiting nonprofits in Los Angeles and Williamsburg. Roundhouse created two different spaces in two very different areas that promoted and enhanced the adidas brand as well as the Urban Outfitters' brand. The concept worked and was successfully adapted to the two unlike spaces.

DESIGN CREDITS:

Design:	Roundhouse, Portland, Oregon, USA Joe Sundby: Creative Director Kate Terrill: Producer / Accounts Justin Smith: Art Director Dana Bainbridge: Design Director Chris Bodven: Designer Beatrice Thompson: Designer Kyle Sundby: Copywriter
Client:	adidas
Artist:	Jason Woodside
Photography:	Matt Dutile / Courtesy of Roundhouse, Portland, Oregon, USA

◀ **Figure 1:** Introducing the adidas pop-up shop and the colorful imagery created for the installation are some sculptural elements that either carry the message or the adidas trefoil logo.

◀ **Figure 2:** The street artist, Jason Woodside, working with the Roundhouse team, "transformed an underground lair into a sub-terranean suite of shopping and celebration." Reclaimed materials balance the adidas Originals white and blue to create a visually clean palette.

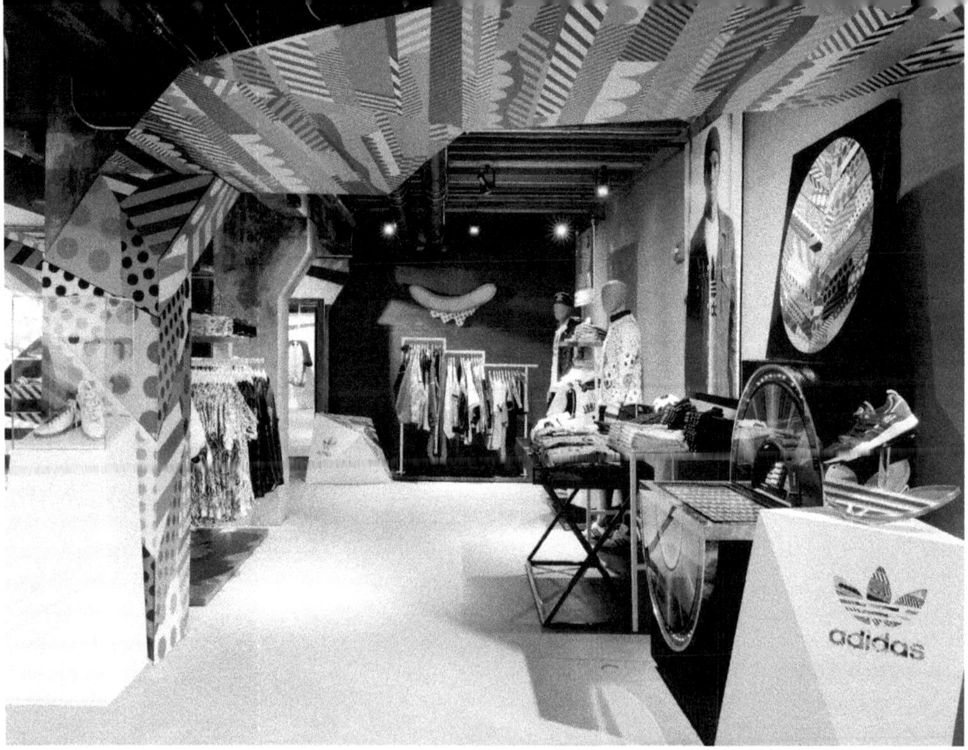

◀ **Figure 3:** Jason Woodside's colorful geometric patterns appear throughout the space. Here his piece climbs from a museum case with an Original adidas sport shoe across the ceiling to connect with a highly decorated jukebox. Pops of color and authentic street settings all come into play.

◀ **Figure 4:** The lounge is an oasis within the Urban Outfitters' Williamsburg store. It offers "the consumer an opportunity to be immersed in a more extensive experience with props and fixtures that evoke the hip hop/NYC/basketball scene and localize the global brand influences." Note the fixture on the far right.

◀ **Figure 5:** A close-up look at the main shoe display, which replicates the adidas trefoil logo. The colorful artwork transforms the simple unit into an eye-filling spectacle and carries a display of featured adidas sports shoes.

◀ **Figure 6:** A view of the Los Angeles pop-up shop at Space 15 Twenty. Here a similar feature unit sets the look in the lounge area, with daylight filling the space from overhead and the numerous windows. The Jason Woodside art fills the space and ties the two pop-up shops together across the country.

PART 4

CASE STUDIES

A Brand Statement

People do shop by brands and brand familiarity does help increase sales. The number of people who shop by brand has increased and more and more shoppers are drawn to brands they recognize or have heard about. Robert Passikoff, president of Brand Keys, a New York-based brand and research consultancy, wrote: "The more considered a purchase, the greater the role a strong brand plays in the decision making process, especially in the very personal category of fashion, where the brand is the source of emotional engagement, and a surrogate for added-on value that engenders positive behavior toward one brand versus another." However, it is in the shop, the restaurant, the showroom, or the trade show space where the brand is enhanced by emotional elements and appeals to the senses, where the brand's image or identity is firmly established in the shopper's mind.

Designing a retail space is not merely focused on the presentation of product: it should also include enhancing the brand experience. According to the Retail Design Institute, store designs can transport shoppers into the world of the brand:

> *Studies have shown that consumers' purchasing behavior is often driven by story-telling and emotions. Information gathered through the senses piques our interest, triggering a strong emotional response that overcomes rational thinking. The result is a heightened experience for the consumer—and increased sales for the store. An immersive retail*

environment can be created using fixtures, layout, music and sound, lighting and even air quality—fragrance or temperature.

In this section of the book we have included a variety of established brands that are creating brand experiences in their stores or restaurants. Karl Lagerfeld's new boutique in Paris was a great success and the designers of that boutique were invited to design the new **KARL LAGERFELD** flagship store in London on prestigious Regent Street. Using the signature elements in new and fitting ways, they created a setting that says "Karl Lagerfeld" as much as the silhouette Lagerfeld profile—ponytail and all—that appears on walls in the minimalistic, black, grated white setting. As the designer explains, "The overall store concept bears reference to the characteristic handwriting of Karl Lagerfeld and is inspired by the vision of the designer." It is a classic example of making a defining design statement.

Cortefiel has for over 75 years stood for quality and style, and what started out as the manufacturing of fine men's suits has now expanded beyond men's fashions to women's clothing, and from tailored clothing to fashion clothing and accessories. The designers at JGA now had to interpret the brand in a series of boutique-like settings that would show off the several different Cortefiel sub-brands in one space and yet maintain the essence of the Cortefiel brand.

For Pennant & Triumph to create another winning retail shop for the popular **Rodd & Gunn** menswear chain, it meant creating "a light summer feeling to the lodge theme" that had been used in Rodd & Gunn's other stores. It had to express "relaxed, authentic, natural and quality"—the four words that, to the designers, best expressed the company's brand.

The **Camper** Company makes each store or showroom an artistic and unique statement of the brand. We are showing a Camper store on Fifth Avenue and a Camper showroom in Shanghai to show how, though different and unique, the essence of the Camper brand comes through. "The design of the Camper showroom in Shanghai was inspired by the urban context of its surroundings. Its spatial qualities and its vibrancy are very characteristic of life in a typical Shanghai alleyway." A spokesperson for Camper Shoes explains: "We seek innovation through our products but also through communication, our stores, etc. To achieve this, Camper collaborates with international designers to create new products and stores. Every design is the direct result of an inherent commitment to creativity."

Swarovski called upon Tokujin Yoshioka, the Japanese designer/architect who has created retail spaces for the company, to design their exhibition stand for the trade fair Baselworld. The designer said: "Swarovski's history of luminance with its pursuit of beauty is part of the Swarovski DNA that I used to design the stand. My intention was to express the space by the dazzle of light—and not by forms. Visitors will enter the world of Swarovski by being veiled with light of luminance."

When the recently opened **Ben Sherman** store opened on Carnaby Street in London, it was like a return to home because in many ways this was where it all began. The designers "wanted to move away from the literal interpretation of 'mod' culture, and take a more subtle and premium approach. We looked at all aspects of the 1960s modernist design to build a visual language reflecting the era of the brand's birth." Throughout, the designers relied on elements of the brand's heritage for decor and for historical reference.

Baccarat's statement begins out on Madison Avenue with its patterned façade. The main purpose of the design was "to underscore the brand's high end heritage and to solidify Baccarat as a contemporary international lifestyle brand"—even if it had 250 years of French tradition and heritage. A look at the design proves it can be done.

Casa Palacio is part of the Palacio de Hierro chain of luxury department stores in Mexico. The goal for the architect/designer was to redesign the home emporium to attract its target market of increasingly affluent Mexican consumers. As the architect concluded, "The style of the store was important in setting the right tone for the brand. We 'merged' classic vocabulary with modern elements. We have designed a shopping environment where customers feel transported and can see themselves using products in their own homes or even envision their new home."

Though Anton Assaad's three previous showrooms for his **Great Dane** branded Danish furniture were effective and successful, he felt they still "lacked the essential element that makes good retail spaces great." The designer of the new space, Gary McCartney, said: "Our main task became to find an idea that would bring the Great Dane brand to life within the space but not compete with the merchandise itself, which is the focus of the showroom." The final concept was based on the reason the shoppers came to Great Dane: quality and craftsmanship.

The Munich-based FC Bayern soccer team is well known and beloved by soccer fans, and especially in Munich. When Wolfgang Gruschwitz was called upon to design the **FC Bayern Fan Shop** in the local stadium, he was asked to "create a unique design with a high emotional quotient and a clear identification of the brand." The dominant red and white color scheme immediately recalls the team's colors and the graphics and blow-ups add a sense of excitement to the many branded items.

A brand is a brand but it is the addition of emotional and sensual values that make the brand memorable in the marketplace. We have mentioned only several of the brands that have restated their brand's position and theme with the creation of their brand identity.

CASE STUDY 4.1

KARL LAGERFELD LONDON

REGENT STREET, LONDON, UK

DESIGN: PLAJER & FRANZ STUDIO, BERLIN, GERMANY / KARL LAGERFELD

DESIGN OBJECTIVE

The design team at plajer & franz studio of Berlin, working with Karl Lagerfeld, the internationally known fashion designer, created the new KARL LAGERFELD concept store on the Boulevard St. Germaine in Paris. Now, this award-winning design has been adapted and introduced as the KARL LAGERFELD flagship store on Regent Street in London. The store spans nearly 2700 sq. ft over two floors and combines the brand's accessible luxury collection with cutting-edge digital technology. Overall it is stamped with Lagerfeld's iconic design aesthetic. Like the Parisian store, according to Werner Franz, CEO and co-founder of the plajer & franz design firm, "it bears reference to the characteristic handwriting of Karl Lagerfeld and is inspired by the vision of the designer and is marked by a minimalistic design with French flair." Franz continues: "The main focus lies in reduction—black and white as well as strong contrasts in shapes and surfaces, blending edgy modern and classic elements. For all that, the rich contrast design of the store appears harmonious and captivates with its love of detail."

DESIGN SOLUTION

Since the concept has been inspired by the vision of—and with the active participation of—Karl Lagerfeld himself, it is the "brand" creating its own brand identity. Franz explains: "It is important that the brand knows itself. Store design is a form of communication and it simply does not work without knowing the brand inside and out. With KARL LAGERFELD, the black and white images and the minimalistic and simple design reflect the DNA of the brand."

In describing what was done in this new retail concept, Werner Franz says:

> *Materials and their surfaces play a vital role in the shop design, often creating multidimensional, reflecting surfaces such as glass and mirror contrasted with matte materials. They allow a play with perspective and create subtle visual illusions—a creative wink and a detail only becomes visible on second sight.*

By cleverly juxtaposing and allowing classic and modern elements to interact, Karl Lagerfeld's and the brand's modern attitude is further reflected.

Franz adds: "Lighting is an important means for creating the theatrical atmosphere and is a crucial aspect of store architecture. Differentiated light levels are used all over the space. It is placed and adjusted so as to accentuate certain elements and highlight important areas. Of course, it is used to highlight the star (the product) and create an adequate stage for it." Adding a special interest and unique quality to the contemporary design is the "digital experience—the virtual window to KARL LAGERFELD." Shoppers, using iPads that are integrated into the display racks, can explore the entire collection on the KARL LAGERFELD website. They can check out the lookbooks or even "communicate with the designer himself via a digital guest book." The built-in touch screens in the dressing rooms encourage shoppers to photograph themselves and share their new looks with their friends via Twitter, Facebook, or e-mail. "It goes without saying that the Karl-community is connected."

CONCLUSION

Says Franz: "The new store is positioned as trend-focused, and as an accessible luxury brand with ready-to-wear and accessories for men and women, and the concept leverages Karl Lagerfeld's iconic image"—branded, sealed, and delivered in style.

DESIGN CREDITS:

Design:	Artistic Direction: Karl Lagerfeld, Paris
	Olaf Becker: Retail Director
Store Design and Design Concept:	plajer & franz studio, Berlin, Germany
	Werner Franz, CEO and Founder: Project Manager
	Sophie Gatzke
	Laird + Partners, New York City, New York, USA
Shopfitting:	Vizona West GmbH, Langenfeld, Germany
Lighting:	Ansorg GmbH, Muehlheim an der Ruhr, Germany
Photography:	plajer & franz studio, Berlin, Germany. © KARL LAGERFELD

▲ **Figure 1:** Located on the well-known fashion street in London—Regent Street—is the new KARL LAGERFELD flagship store. The noted and recognizable Karl Lagerfeld profile makes a strong impact in one window while the other opens to a view of the shop.

▶ **Figure 2:** Outline blue Images of Karl Lagerfeld watch over the shop, adding a decorative note to the sleek, neutral setting. "With Karl Lagerfeld, the black and white images and the minimalistic and simple design reflect the DNA of the brand."

◀ **Figure 3:** "The main function lies in reduction—black and white as well as strong contrasts in shapes and surfaces, blending edgy modern and classic elements." The fabulous mural on the back wall is by ilovedust, a British design group who have collaborated with Karl Lagerfeld on previous store and design projects.

◀ **Figure 4:** Mirrors, glass, and reflective surfaces contrast with matte areas to create the exciting look for the shop. Elegant black abstract mannequins wear the featured garments in the soft gray-walled room.

▶ **Figure 5:** A classic black marble fireplace with a mirror over it adds a warm and inviting quality to the room with its unique chairs and black fixtures and displayers.

◀ **Figure 6:** A stairway leads down to the men's area on the lower level. The same black and white palette is used here as well as the simple fixturing and mirrors and reflective surfaces.

◀ **Figure 7:** In the almost all-black room, the Karl Lagerfeld signature profile watches over the display of men's accessories and gift items.

▶ **Figure 8:** Oversized graphics—mainly black and white—appear throughout the store. They are blow-ups of current LAGERFELD ads that appear in top fashion publications.

CASE STUDY 4.2

BEN SHERMAN

CARNABY STREET, LONDON, UK

DESIGN: BRINKWORTH, LONDON, UK

DESIGN OBJECTIVE

Ben Sherman was born in England in 1925, migrated to the United States in 1945, and then returned to London where in 1963 he designed and made the shirts that would become the mainstay of the Ben Sherman brand. The "shirt" was based on the classic American Ivy League shirt and, with additions that included "his feel and passion for fabric, pattern and color," he created a unique garment. The company's website adds: "Color was something that particularly intrigued Ben, so he used Oxford fabrics in pale shades of pink, yellow and blue. He used candy stripes, again, using pale pinks, greens and blues. He wanted the best fabrics, so the special fabrics were all from America. The shirts were a huge success, offering something brand new and previously unseen in England." The shirt was "revolutionary" and picked up by the Mods—the young, cool, and swinging young men of 1960s London—and by 1963 Ben Sherman had a shop on what would become the icon of the Mod movement: Carnaby Street.

The new store on Carnaby Street was designed by the Brinkworth design consultancy under the direction of the CEO, Adam Brinkworth. According to Adam,

> *Ben Sherman (the client company) briefed us to build on the heritage of modernism and improve the product stories around the range to highlight to the customer the provenance of the garments. The Ben Sherman team wanted to move away from the literal interpretation of "mod" culture, and take a more subtle and premium approach. We looked at all aspects of the 1960s modernist design to build a visual language reflecting the era of the brand's birth. Our interpretation of the brand has meant that the new retail concept now attracts a much wider and diverse audience while still remaining relevant to the loyal Ben Sherman followers.*

DESIGN SOLUTION

Brinkworth and his design team produced a store concept that references British icons such as traditional pubs and the London Underground. The Carnaby Street façade shows the influences of the Victorian warehouses that surround the Ben Sherman headquarters in the EC1 area of London and features teapot-brown glazed bricks combined with black and white tiles. A pneumatically controlled, moving rail system dominates the window space with an unending parade of Ben Sherman shirts—the core product of the brand. The viewer on the street gets to see the moving spectacle of the garments from all angles, and reeded glass around the display feature offers a diffused look into the shop.

Inside the shop the look continues with concrete floors accented in key areas by reclaimed oak parquet flooring. The walls are covered with authentic glazed Victorian tiles enhanced with molded dado rails, curved corner pieces and the iconic teapot-brown glazed bricks introduced on the shop's façade. "This limited material and color palette establishes a strong brand character—creating a muted backdrop on which to display the collection," adds Brinkworth.

The heritage and history of the brand is presented at the top of the stairs by a wall created from rolls of original Ben Sherman fabrics—preserved behind glass. This "highlights the heritage of the brand and adds pattern and color to the interior." This decorative application is repeated around the fitting rooms in the basement.

Throughout, custom-designed and traditionally produced display units, based on British mid-twentieth-century furniture, mirror the detailing of the clothing. Mid-floor furniture pieces are used as focal displays, while the shelving and hanging rails provide maximum flexibility in the presentation of lifestyle visual merchandising.

The focal piece and the centerpiece of the design is the Shirt Bar that is located at the rear of the store. Leading the way are custom-made architectural light boxes. An under-lit mid-floor counter and a very full wall display of shirts in the Shirt Bar are "dedicated to shirting and designed as an opportunity for the brand to showcase its breadth of knowledge in every aspect of shirting while it offers the customer an immersive brand experience."

CONCLUSION

The store won "Best Fashion Retail Interior of the Year" and has proven itself very successful as a draw for the desired clientele. Adam Brinkworth says: "Following the initial design development and implementation of the new retail concept, we are continuing our work with Ben Sherman for the rollout of the concept in multiple international locations."

DESIGN CREDITS:

Design:	Brinkworth
	Adam Brinkworth: CEO; Murray Aitkin, Sonny Cant, Sam Derrick
Client:	Ben Sherman
	Pan Philippou, Mark Maidment, Rod Cameron, Martin Morris
Photography:	Louise Melchior

◀ **Figure 1:** The Carnaby Street façade shows the influence of the Victorian warehouses that surround the Ben Sherman headquarters and features teapot brown glazed bricks combined with black and white tiles. A revolving display of shirts fills the windows.

▶ **Figure 3:** Original rolls of Ben Sherman shirting fabrics are preserved and displayed in glass cases at the top of the stairs leading down to the Shirt Bar. This is the heritage and history of the brand and it also adds color and pattern to the shop's monochromatic palette.

▶ **Figure 4:** The Shirt Bar. On the left is one of the cases with the heritage rolls of fabric. This decorative motif is repeated around the fitting rooms in the basement, adding color and pattern.

◀ **Figure 2:** The custom-designed display fixtures are based on British mid-twentieth-century furniture and mirror the detailing on the Ben Sherman clothing. The mid-floor units serve as focal pieces and the simple rod and shelving wall units provide maximum flexibility.

▲ **Figure 5:** The Shirt Bar is the centerpiece of the store. The full wall display of folded shirts and the under-lit illuminated unit with hung shirts "offer the customer an immersive brand experience."

CASE STUDY 4.3

RODD & GUNN

NOOSA, AUSTRALIA

DESIGN: PENNANT & TRIUMPH, AUCKLAND, NEW ZEALAND

DESIGN OBJECTIVE

What began in 1946 as a shirt made in New Zealand, with an English Pointer dog as its logo, has since developed into an international brand that, according to the website, has "a strong and loyal following in Australia and almost iconic status in New Zealand. In addition there is an unusually high international customer base particularly in stores with high tourist traffic such as Noosa in Australia and places such as Queenstown in New Zealand. There is a significant following amongst American, English and European tourists who 'discover' the brand while traveling and want to continue the Rodd & Gunn experience upon returning home." And—it isn't just shirts anymore: Rodd & Gunn now covers all aspects of a modern man's wardrobe. The brand statement concludes: "The brand philosophy is to create clothes that draw the best from nature in its purest state. Hence the focus on using linens, cottons, wools and leathers that are soft, practical, superbly textured and durable. The result is clothing and accessories that are completely modern, yet firmly grounded in the brand's core values." According to Justin Roderique of the Auckland-based architectural firm of Pennant & Triumph—the design firm that created this and other Rodd & Gunn spaces—"Four key words would summarize the brand: relaxed, authentic, natural and quality." And that was what the Rodd & Gunn client was to perceive upon entering the store in this resort town. As the English Pointer logo suggests, Rodd & Gunn is all about casual clothes imbued with the essence of the New Zealand great outdoors.

DESIGN SOLUTION

The "lodge" theme seems to be the natural expression and setting for the brand, with its natural materials and feeling of the semi-rugged, masculine lifestyle. To create the desired light summer feeling, Roderique continues:

> *The Noosa store was designed to capture the ambience of a New Zealand summer beach retreat or lodge and as such incorporate beach materials such as a "board and batten"*

exterior with large barn or shed-like doors. The lodge concept ties back to the brand's values with its use of authentic and masculine materials. To further enhance that summer feel on the interior, we used a number of elements that combine to create a truly exceptional tropical experience.

This is no shack or lean-to or makeshift construction; this is an upscale, gentleman's sort of space. Stepping in from the black exterior accented in white to the almost all-white interior is a revelation. The shopper steps into a gentleman's retreat: a casual home from home with whitewashed wooden floors and tongue-and-groove wood paneled walls, painted white. With assorted ceiling heights and the space divided into "rooms," the feeling of a dwelling rather than a retail store is further enhanced. The white wall battens and the wooden shutters that add a textural statement to the palette, along with the furnishings in warm, natural wood, are almost signature statements as they recall the shop designed for Rodd & Gunn by Pennant & Triumph in Sylvia Park, New Zealand. Whirring about—way overhead—adding a soft, white noise along with the gentle breeze, are the plantation fans. They also become part of the look and feel of the space. There are organic sisal rugs on select areas of the wood floor while an occasional wall will pick up the same warm, neutral biscuit color in the woven grass wallpapers used to sheathe these areas. Providing comfort and atmosphere are the white cane chairs, natural woven wicker baskets and trunks, and the live potted palm trees—green and adding a sparkling color accent. Many of the graphics that appear on the walls are framed in white as well. Garments are presented in open "wardrobes" or in niches in the walls. The occasional headless mannequin shows up dressed in a Rodd & Gunn outfit. All together, the ambience is casual, smart, sophisticated, and masculine. Or, to quote Justin Roderique's original brand statement, "Relaxed, authentic, natural and quality."

CONCLUSION

Nic Rush, Group Visual Brand Manager for Rodd & Gunn, sums it up this way: "The aim was for Pennant & Triumph to create a store to match the mood of such a great holiday destination—Noosa in Queensland, Australia. It's a place where the customer can relax, linger and spend more time shopping in privacy and peace, totally able to focus on the product offered within, and Pennant & Triumph have achieved this admirably."

DESIGN CREDITS:

Design:	Pennant & Triumph, Kingsland, Auckland, New Zealand Justin Roderique: Architectural Designer
Client:	Rodd & Gunn Nic Rush: Group Visual Brand Manager
Photography:	Pennant & Triumph

◀ **Figure 1:** The black "board and batten" exterior opens into an almost all-white interior—into a gentleman's retreat. "The lodge concept ties back to the brand's values with its use of authentic and masculine materials."

◀ **Figure 2:** The shop resembles "a casual home from home" with its whitewashed wood floors and "tongue-and-groove" white-painted wood walls. White framed pictures and authentic furniture complete the masculine feel of the space.

▶ **Figure 3:** Adding a textural quality to the shop are the louvered shutters and the white wall battens. Accents of warm, light brown wood add to the "natural" palette.

▶ **Figure 4:** Sisal rugs cover the floors in some places and different ceiling heights add to the illusion of different rooms. Garments are presented in open "wardrobes" or niches carved out of the walls.

◀ **Figure 5:** Adding to the home-like, beach ambience of the shop are the white cane chairs, natural wicker baskets, potted palms, and the ceiling fans whirring overhead.

◀ **Figure 6:** The dressing rooms. A wall-to-wall mirror expands the space while grass cloth on the walls adds another beach texture to the material palette. All together, the palette recalls the brand: "relaxed, authentic, natural and quality."

CASE STUDY 4.4

BACCARAT

MADISON AVENUE, NEW YORK CITY, USA

DESIGN: RAFAEL DE CARDENAS LTD., NEW YORK CITY, USA

DESIGN OBJECTIVE

Baccarat is an outstanding brand for fine crystal that has been available for 250 years. Obviously, history and heritage play very important roles in the Baccarat brand. The company prides itself on its exceptional archives which contain over 200,000 drawings and 65,000 molds since the brand's inception. This statement comes from the company's website: "Baccarat is, more than ever, a symbol of exception, of perfection, distinguished by icons fashioned from breath and exalted by fire. With the support of talented French craftsmen, the crystalworks has drawn inspiration from its roots, its craftsmanship, and its heritage to transmute tradition into creation."

To commemorate that grand birthday, the company called upon the exceptional design talents of Rafael de Cardenas to breathe a new life into their Madison Avenue store and "underscore the brand's high end heritage and solidify Baccarat as a contemporary international lifestyle brand."

DESIGN SOLUTION

The transformation on Madison Avenue to make Baccarat "a visible presence in the luxury world" started with the façade. Rafael de Cardenas, the designer, says:

> *The Madison Avenue store design extracts the delicate yet rigid details of finely cut crystal and executes them in an architectural manner. The store's double-height glass-frit façade features an etched glass pattern inspired by the house's renowned crystal diamond cut, showcasing the brand's French heritage and 250-year history. The array of triangles create a three dimensional illusion on a two dimensional surface.*

Shoppers enter into a grand and majestic two-story entry space and on to a brushed Nordic black granite floor. De Cardenas continues: "Interior entry walls are wrapped in faceted strips of Macassar ebony and mirror. This geometry reflects both the natural light from the façade and tiers of grand crystal chandeliers. Nordic black granite is used as a high contrast backdrop to display Baccarat crystal, while niches of white gold leaf highlight special products." Baccarat now features tableware, chandeliers, decorative objects, carafes, and jewelry.

Throughout the 2500 sq. ft space Rafael de Cardenas has added touches of classical French design like the diamond pattern on the wood flooring and the detailing of the ceiling moldings. Probably the most dramatic feature in the design is the two-story black granite Icon Wall where large-scale products are displayed in an appealing manner. Video panels are inserted into the entryway as well as the Jewelry Bar and they "connect Baccarat's extensive 250-year history with the future—bringing to life Baccarat's storied past of artisanship and luxury."

CONCLUSION

In summing up his design efforts for the brand, de Cardenas says: "The unique application of these signature moves both broadens the brand's appeal to a younger audience while simultaneously highlighting the craftsmanship and heritage of Baccarat crystal and reinforcing their existing client base."

DESIGN CREDITS:

Design:	Rafael de Cardenas, Ltd., New York City, USA Rafael de Cardenas: Principal
Design team:	Rafael de Cardenas, Justin Capuco, Robert Passov, Scott Rominger, Samuel Suttcliffe
Client:	Baccarat
Photography:	Floto + Warner, New York, USA

▲ **Figure 1:** The etched pattern on the two-story glass façade recalls Baccarat's crystal diamond cut and introduces the brand's French heritage.

◀ **Figure 2:** The shop as seen from the vast entryway. Faceted strips of Macassar ebony are combined with panels of mirror to create a unique and dramatic wall finish.

◀ **Figure 3:** The French heritage of the brand is reinforced in the French architectural details like the wood patterned floor and the ceiling molding details.

▶ **Figure 5:** A closer look at the faceted wall finish and the Baccarat crystal chandeliers that add sparkling light touches to the interior. Chrome-accented shadow boxes, set into or extending out from the wall, feature special crystal items.

◀ **Figure 4:** Illuminated from within, crystal-covered columns lead into a dark wood area of the shop. A high shine chromed fixture is the focal element in the space.

CASE STUDY 4.5

CORTEFIEL

SEVILLE, SPAIN

DESIGN: JGA, SOUTHFIELD, MICHIGAN, USA

DESIGN OBJECTIVE

The Cortefiel Group is a leading European fashion retailer that is made up of four brands: Cortefiel, Springfield, women'secret, and Pedro del Hierro. With the addition of its outlet chain, Fifty Factory, the Group is present and very successful in 65 countries. The brief that was presented to JGA of Southfield, Michigan was "to add life and iconicity to the brand, lending a sense of energy, renewal, and innovation to inspire its core customer and to expand the brand's demographic and psychographic target."

DESIGN SOLUTION

Kenneth Nisch, Chairman of JGA and a leader of the design team for this project along with the Creative Director, Michael Curtis, explains: "The history of this business is primarily manufacturing of fine men's suits. Over the years, the company's mission and platform has expanded beyond men's fashions to women's—from tailored clothing to fashion clothing, accessories, etc. The key point of differentiation is exactly this heritage of tailoring and clothing making, versus a more traditional retailer that is a distribution arm for other people's things. Think of the traditional department store. Much focus is put on looking at ways to merchandise that are contemporary and lifestyle focused, but also can draw from its roots, from the traditional haberdasher. In looking at a brand brief, in most cases you are focused on implicit versus explicit cues, and in the sum total of the subtlety of these cues, are quite powerful versus having to make a sign that basically talks about the brand and the brand's mission."

Nisch goes on to explain some of the "subtle cues" adopted in designing this 7800 sq. ft Cortefiel store in Seville that was conceived to house all the Group's brands. The "subtlety" was used to define and delineate the different brands and yet create a flowing and homogeneous space:

> *There are both implicit and explicit aspects of the store design. For instance, the back area is rustic, eclectic, and collected, with more sense of freedom—permission for the consumer to mix and match. There is more cross-*

integration between men's and women's products where denim is the focus. But it is not unheard of to see a range of denim jeans displayed with a cashmere jacket and a polo shirt, giving "permission" to the consumer to mix-and-match and self-create in ways that may be less appreciated in the more formal areas of the store where products tend to be more organized around classification and a bit more hand sewn. In the more bespoke area, the inspiration is more mid-century modernism. There is a certain slickness, subtlety, and quietness to the character of the fixtures and the displays, giving a sense of "appropriateness."

The more tailored and casual areas are defined and balanced as a "dance" between architecture, fixtures, environmental fixtures, lighting, and visual techniques that give an impression of both continuity and diversity among sub-brands.

For this prototype, the designers at JGA created a series of "proprietary touchpoints" to differentiate between the fashion-forward and classic sub-brands. Spiraling chrome display fixtures add an organic quality to the design and a new contemporary style to the brand, as do other molded and organic forms, cantilevers, and materials that "stretch the functional design parameters of traditional European retailers." The organic shapes serve to help shoppers move through the space while the creation of zones defines the dressy casual from the weekend wear. Casual zones have exposed ceilings and curved walls and this format of zones also allows the multi-brands to work together. A neutral color palette is used throughout, with splashes of color to highlight and differentiate areas. These "splashes" appear in the accent wall coverings, floor materials, and in the textures used.

Because this is a prototype for the Cortefiel stores of the future, Ken Nisch says that it was designed as a "kit-of-parts." "The kit-of-parts are very flexible to deal with in the more pragmatic aspects of execution." Depending upon the country or city where the new store will go, it is possible "to adapt—in terms of dialing up or dialing down its formal versus casual, women's versus men's, and how the store itself can be pulled together across various square footages while still communicating the brand essence. There is also the ability through the 'soft experience' to dial up the company's heritage. This can be done primarily through graphics, visual merchandising, display and digital media, within the physical framework of the store prototype."

CONCLUSION

The store in Seville has experienced double-digit increases in sales and, according to Ken Nisch, has "broadened the demographic appeal particularly related to age and has higher branding marks relative to be seen as a specialty department store rather than a 'big' small box store."

DESIGN CREDITS:

Design:	JGA, Southfield, Michigan, USA Kenneth Nisch: Chairman Michael Curtis: Creative Director
Client:	Cortefiel Fernando Saenz: Cortefiel and Pedro del Hierro General Manager Enrique Fernandez del Riego: Cortefiel and Pedro del Hierro Operations Manager Tomas Romero: Cortefiel and Pedro del Hierro Visual Merchandising Manager Jordi Allepuz: Visual Director, Grupo Cortefiel Paula Aza: Design and Works Manager
Architect:	Javier Parras, Madrid, Spain
General Contractor:	Indibu Construcciones, Madrid, Spain
Lifestyle/Graphics Photography:	Grupo Rafael, Madrid, Spain
Store Photography:	Paco Alorda Fotógrafo, Madrid, Spain

◀ **Figure 1:** The Cortefiel store in Seville is a "house of brands and sub-brands": designed with proprietary touchpoints to distinguish the fashion-forward from the classic.

◀ **Figure 2:** The organic, free-flowing feel of the Casual area is seen in the partial ceiling drop over open ceilings and sweeping floor lines. These shapes facilitate shoppers' movement through the different spaces of the store.

◀ **Figure 3:** Denims are a popular Cortefiel item and this area contains the popular brands artfully arranged on built-up display tables and in wall cabinets.

◀ **Figure 4:** Bronze-toned abstract mannequins appear throughout the different areas dressed to show the mix-and-match possibilities of the garments.

◀ **Figure 5:** In the women's area the curved walls add to the organic quality of the design. An occasional colored wall adds a touch of drama and distinction.

▶ Figure 6:
The warm, beige color feeling fills the women's area. The cash/wrap desk is accentuated by a large colored graphic and the soft green color that highlights other walls.

▶ Figure 7:
The spiraling chrome fixtures, here swirling around a column, add an organic quality to the design and a new contemporary style to the top Pedro del Hierro brand.

◀ **Figure 8:** The use of molded and organic forms, cantilevers, and new materials add quality to the Cortefiel brand and go well beyond the parameters used by traditional European retailers. This new, fresh approach has had a definite appeal for the trendy young shoppers of Seville.

CASE STUDY 4.6

CAMPER FIFTH AVENUE

FIFTH AVENUE, NEW YORK, USA

DESIGN: NENDO, TOKYO, JAPAN

DESIGN OBJECTIVE

The fourth Camper shoe store opened on Fifth Avenue near 44th Street in New York City, and bears little relationship in design to any of the others in New York or around the world. However, parts of this new concept, designed by the Japanese design firm Nendo, appear in the Serrano shop in Madrid. The Camper brand, as described by the company itself, is as follows:

> *One of the brand statements is indeed heritage; we are a shoe company for more than 135 years (since 1877) and very loyal to our Mediterranean roots, but, at the same time, we seek innovation through our product but also through our communication and our stores. Every design is the direct result of an inherent commitment to creativity and our shoes are designed to be comfortable, long-lasting, and imaginative. To achieve this, Camper also cooperates with international designers to create new products, stores, and our two Casa Camper hotels. Every design is the direct result of an inherent commitment to creativity. The Camper shop doesn't reflect our place of origin (the island of Majorca) nor our immediate surroundings, but is created to exist in a new global culture.*

DESIGN SOLUTION

This 1250 sq. ft store (with an additional 600 sq. ft for storage) has all the hallmarks of the minimalist Nendo design and its lead designer, Oki Sato. This is not a new relationship of client and designer; that began several years ago with a trade show stand that appeared at an international fashion event in Barcelona. Following that outing, Nendo went on to design a variety of Camper stores in Osaka, Paris, San Francisco, and Moscow, "with the same exquisite subtlety" and a concept that has been enlarged upon in the new, larger space. With regard to the new store, shown here, Oki Sato said: "We've created a new concept for larger Camper stores in which the shoes 'are walking on air,' which is based on a previous idea developed in smaller stores. When designing such a big space you have to face the challenge of how to use the upper half of the walls to display the shoes in areas with such high ceilings. Our new approach involves making white resin models of the Pelotas shoe—one of Camper's most iconic styles—and decorating the walls with them to fill the space and create the feel of an orderly stockroom."

The startling "art installation" look of the space is evident out on the heavily trafficked Fifth Avenue, where this shop is surrounded by some of the world's most well-known fashion brands. The stark white on white of the space and its high ceiling and the endless number of white resin Pelotas shoes climbing, climbing, climbing is contrasted with the neutral gray of the concrete floors, the gray cabinets and simple benches, and the low platforms where the assorted styles of shoes are displayed in the same geometric order. Popping out and making a big and intended statement is the cube-like cash/wrap desk finished in Camper's signature red color. Everything about the space and its furnishings underplays the understated minimalism of the Nendo design.

CONCLUSION

The "Together" concept is part of the Camper brand and this store—like the many other Camper stores around the world—is evidence that the concept is alive and working. Says Miguel Fluxa, CEO of Camper: "Throughout its history Camper's personality as reflected in its stores has always been enriched by the contributions of designers, architects, and artists. Since 2006 (when the concept was 'written down'), the projects developed together with the Bouroullec brothers, Jaime Hayon, Alfredo Haberli, amongst others, in different cities of the world show that Camper opts for new ways to communicate the essence of a brand that is always loyal to its original spirit."

DESIGN CREDITS:

Design:	Nendo, Tokyo, Japan
	Oki Sato and Akihiro Ito: Co-founders of Nendo
Client:	Camper
	Miguel Fluxa: CEO
Photography:	Daici Ano. Courtesy of Camper Shoes

◀ **Figure 1:** The international brand Camper opened its newest New York City shoe store on Fifth Avenue, designed by the minimalist architectural firm Nendo. The store looks more like a gallery than a retail setting.

◀ **Figure 2:** Each Camper store is unique and different and does not reflect the brand's Mediterranean origins but is "created to exist in a new global culture." The brand's signature colors of red and white are constant.

◤ **Figure 3:** To tie in with the "walking on air" theme and the store's high ceilings, the designers filled the walls with hundreds of white resin forms of the brand's Pelotas shoe. The white forms climb the stark white walls.

◀ **Figure 4:** The fixturing consists of gray cabinets, low white platforms, and simple benches all arranged, like the sample shoes, in geometric order. On the wall some forms with featured shoes replace the white Pelotas shoe for greater emphasis.

▲ **Figure 5:** The simple, cube-like cash/wrap desk blazes in the Camper signature red and, though off in the rear of the store, it is clearly visible and reiterates the red of the store's façade. Seating is provided in the blacked-out niches in the white walls.

CASE STUDY 4.7

CAMPER SHANGHAI

SHANGHAI, CHINA

DESIGN: NERI & HU, SHANGHAI, CHINA

DESIGN OBJECTIVE

When Lyndon Neri and Rossana Hu, founders and leading architects and designers of Neri & Hu Design and Research of Shanghai, were invited by the Camper company to design their new showroom in Shanghai, they were given "carte blanche to maintain their own personal style." Over the past years Camper has surrounded itself with leading designers and architects to create unique and exclusive stores. (See the Camper Fifth Avenue case study in this collection.) The other briefing point that the design team was given was to preserve the local aesthetics.

Lyndon Neri goes on to explain: "Camper is best known for its iconic designs and flair for creating unique concepts in both footwear and retail shop design. Camper wanted to integrate this new showroom space within the surroundings of the Shanghai French Concession area, which has a remarkable, distinct character from the ultra-modern Shanghai. It boasts multiple small alleys and old houses."

DESIGN SOLUTION

"The spatial qualities of the building and its vibrancy are very characteristic of life in a typical Shanghai alleyway, known locally as a 'nong-tang.' We've extended the entrance from the street right into the showroom area—producing a physical cross-section of the building, as if it were an area of a house, which creates a meeting space that can also be used to hold presentations and conferences. We've included a mirrored surface at the end of the entrance way which creates the impression of a much longer cross-sectional area and gives the idea of the newly constructed building having been inserted into the old industrial warehouse."

Rossana Hu picks up the story of how the brand identity was achieved:

> *The urban context is also reflected in the materials we've used. The building structure is made from reclaimed wooden frames sourced locally, and gray bricks used as filler material. The reclaimed wood comes from demolished houses in the alleyways and*

reveals its origins and the passage of time through the patina of paint, newspapers, and painted papers that remain stuck onto the frames.

Besides the wooden frames and the gray bricks, red (lining the main frame and the staircase + the custom-created Solo Chair with special edition red legs) and white (for the walls) are of course key colors/elements reflecting Camper's corporate colors. Camper's signature red "bridge" logo is subtly placed on the windows and at the entrance. We've added a hint of playfulness by hanging some of Camper's most signature shoes from the ceiling. A skylight adds to the feeling of being in an outside alleyway, and throughout the day long linear shadows are cast by the shoes.

In addition, the architects created other furniture pieces for this project such as the shelving and the "Lazy Susan" table in the pressroom.

CONCLUSION

In summing up the result of their design efforts, Neri says: "Camper is not only about shoes, it's about uniqueness, the capability of integrating through design, communication and creative know-how within different cultures into a select global marketplace, and I think we have succeeded in that."

As to how effective this design of the Camper showroom is for the Camper brand, Miguel Fluxa, CEO of Camper, has this to say: "This is the first time we've worked together with Neri & Hu and our first opening in Shanghai. This won't most likely be a prototype design since we've tried to capture the local culture and surroundings through design, different cultures, and creative know-how. We love the end result and what Neri & Hu did with the space and we are looking forward to collaborating together again in the future."

DESIGN CREDITS:

Design:	Neri & Hu Design and Research Office (NHDRO), Shanghai, China Lyndon Neri and Rossana Hu: Founders and lead architects
Client:	Camper Miguel Fluxa: CEO
Photography:	Shen Zhongahi

▶ **Figure 1:** With respect to its surroundings—and the narrow alleyways of this part of Shanghai—the architects extended the entrance from the street into the showroom.

▶ **Figure 2:** Seen beyond the steps is the showroom area with sample shoes on display along the open perimeter walls. Lighting fixtures are suspended over the work tables.

◀ **Figure 3:** White walls and Camper red accents along with the Camper steps create the unique two-story interior of the showroom.

◀ **Figure 4:** The urban context is reflected in the materials used in the construction. The reclaimed wood comes from demolished houses in the alleyways and gray bricks are used as filler material.

◀ **Figure 5:** The hallway approaching the open space. The open shelves, on the right, are part of the showroom area with featured shoes on display.

▶ **Figure 6:** The skylight adds to the feeling of being out in an alleyway while the suspended signature Camper shoes add "a hint of playfulness" to the reclaimed wood and gray brick structure.

CASE STUDY 4.8

GREAT DANE

REDFERN, SYDNEY, AUSTRALIA

DESIGN: McCARTNEY DESIGN, SYDNEY, AUSTRALIA

DESIGN OBJECTIVE

Anton Assaad has a passion for classic and modern Scandinavian furniture, homeware, and lighting and he has established three showrooms in Australia in the past six years. During that time he has built a loyal following of Scandinavian design devotees. Although he was happy with the brand that he has built and the showrooms in Sydney and Melbourne, he felt that they still lacked that essential element that makes a good retail space. Great Dane furniture speaks for itself. It is beautifully designed, simple and classic, and manufactured with painstaking care in Scandinavia. Seemingly, the missing part of the equation was the customer—why does the Great Dane customer pay a premium for having the real thing from Denmark when they can easily buy inexpensive replicas of Italian and American designs? In a survey of Great Dane customers Anton Assaad found that customers were impressed by Great Dane's passion for design, the enthusiasm of the sales staff, and the sense that they were getting a prestigious product—not because of the high price tag but because of the beauty and uniqueness of the product.

Gary McCartney of McCartney Design of Sydney, who had designed the other showrooms, explains what happened in designing the newest showroom: "Our main task became to find an idea that would bring the Great Dane brand to life within the space but not compete with the merchandise itself, which is the focus of the showroom."

DESIGN SOLUTION

We considered several ideas but the final concept was based on something that customers considered their main reason for shopping there: quality, craftsmanship, and heritage. We expressed this in-store by selecting pictures of classic Danish designers like Hans Wegner and Finn Juhl and creating translucent room dividers featuring their portraits and philosophies. We focused on the designers and the principles that lie behind their work. To further emphasize the idea of craftsmanship we placed some of the furniture on plinths like works of art, and annotated wall displays to give an art gallery feel. We designed a mirrored plinth so that customers can see that the underside of a chair is indeed as beautifully finished as the visible parts.

Finishes are simple: the whole showroom is painted white, with the sprinkler pipes picked out in red. The timber floor has been whitewashed. Lighting by Bettina Easton at E-Lux was designed to bring the colors in the furniture to life, and a few simple rugs helped to define spaces. The result is a space that perfectly presents the sculptural forms and colors of the furniture. The large translucent panels with the designers' pictures provide authenticity to the brand and serve to create smaller, more intimate spaces to house particular collections. Not only do they divide up the merchandise, they create areas in which customers can slow down and relax. It's a great illustration of the fact that people like to immerse themselves when given the opportunity, and the store planning facilitates this. At the same time, staff can easily see the customers, so there's no danger of them getting "lost."

CONCLUSION

Gary McCartney quotes the Great Dane website: "the Danish word Hygge ['hoo-ga'] describes the deep sense of pleasure found in making ordinary things extraordinary. It's about believing that when everyday objects are beautiful, life is beautiful. This certainly comes across in Great Dane, and we believe we have extended the philosophy to the retail environment that surrounds it."

DESIGN CREDITS:

Design:	McCartney Design, Sydney, Australia
	Gary McCartney: Principal and Design Director
	Bent Patterson: Design team
Client:	Great Dane
	Anton Assaad: Founder and Director
Lighting:	Bettina Easton, E-Lux Lighting Design & Consultancy, Sydney, Australia
Photography:	Steve Back, Sydney, Australia

▲ **Figure 1:** Scandinavian furniture and homeware are featured in the Great Dane Sydney showroom. There is a Danish quality in the simple, all-white ambience that not only plays up the product color but adds to the gallery quality of the space.

◀ **Figure 2:** Each chair is treated like a piece of sculpture with mirrored bases that allow shoppers to appreciate the underside construction as well as the front and side views.

◀ **Figure 3:** Large translucent fabric panels with portraits of notable Danish designers carry out the "quality, craftsmanship, and Danish heritage" essence of the brand for the various pieces made in Denmark.

▶ **Figure 4:** Some of the panels carry quotations that underscore the artistry of Danish design. Pictured here is Hans Wegner and some Wegner-designed furniture.

▶ Figure 5: In addition to the quotations on the dividing panels there are annotated wall displays "to give an art gallery feel" to the showroom.

◀ Figure 6: The sprinkler system is highlighted in red as a decorative note and the lighting system was designed to bring the colors of the furnishings to life. The setting helps make "ordinary things extraordinary."

CASE STUDY 4.9

FC BAYERN FAN SHOP

ALLIANZ ARENA, MUNICH, GERMANY

DESIGN: GRUSCHWITZ GMBH, MUNICH, GERMANY

DESIGN OBJECTIVE

If you are a fan of the Bayern soccer team that plays its home games in the Allianz Arena in Munich, then you know what "mia san mia" means. It is the rallying cry of the fans that is also the promise of the team's brand—"we are who we are"—and who they are is *your* team. This is a traditional team and, as Wolfgang Gruschwitz, the architect/designer of this shop loaded with Bayern team-branded merchandise explains, "they have very strong regional roots and FC Bayern represents success at a high international level." It is probably the most successful German soccer team and has a great reputation.

The brief presented to Gruschwitz by the soccer club requested that the shop be unique—"with a high emotional quotient and a clear identification of the FC Bayern Munich brand. On the other hand, the shop should be functional with regard to the special requirements and expectations for a store located in a soccer stadium."

DESIGN SOLUTION

In describing how Gruschwitz and his team approached the design of this shop, Wolfgang Gruschwitz responds:

> *What makes the special emotional atmosphere of a soccer game? Is it witnessing the adrenaline high of the players and/or the frenzy of the fans? Two things excite the audience: the euphoria of a shot hitting the goal and the dynamism of the team players. The design of a fan store has to create an atmosphere that recalls that excitement—and that is exactly what inspired the planning, conceptualizing, and realization of this FC Bayern store. Also, it is very important to show and to emphasize the image of the brand as well as define who the fans are, where the fans come from, what the club means to them, and what is the club's heritage.*

Since the shop is located "where it is at"—in the arena where the game is played—the shoppers bring that strong emotional high with them into the shop where they are literally immersed in the bright red and white team colors. Gruschwitz elaborates: "As these are rather strong colors, you have to be very sensitive and find the right amount to use and where—too much color confuses the shopper and reduces the 'preciousness' of the store, while too little color might not create the emotions you anticipate as a fan."

The soft, medium-gray color that appears on the highly polished concrete floor and the open, industrial ceiling, along with the crisp white of the walls, ceiling, and laminate-sheathed fixtures, hold the exuberance of the team's signature red in check. The fan who comes in and is "just looking" soon becomes involved with the branded products which are presented to encourage interaction with the shopper. Though the game is being played out in the arena, there are "games" to be played in here, so the "action" never ceases. Gruschwitz explains: "there are large ball chutes, an individual flocking station [where fans can get their garments personalized], and multimedia installations" to encourage customer interaction. The giant blow-ups of the team heroes—in action—add to the emotional climate that Gruschwitz and his team tried so hard to instill in the ambience. The adidas brand gets its own showing in the shop and yet becomes part of the shop's total look. With pulses racing and patience at its lowest, Gruschwitz made checking out for these fans simpler by providing a large, multi-station cash/wrap area.

CONCLUSION

Summing it all up, Wolfgang Gruschwitz says: "There is stylishness, emotionalism, and functionality in the shop's concept—all of which merge to present in perfect harmony the corporate design and brand image."

DESIGN CREDITS:

Design:	Gruschwitz GmbH, Munich, Germany Wolfgang Gruschwitz: Architect/Designer
Client:	FC Bayern
Photography:	Anja Walther / Gruschwitz GmbH

▲ **Figure 1:** FC Bayern's fans know the team's red and white colors and that is what they see in the club's fan shop. The fan's rallying cry of "mia san mia" ("we are who we are") appears on banners throughout the shop.

▲ **Figure 2:** The medium-gray polished concrete floor and white surround serve to highlight the signature red embellished merchandise. Easily moved floor fixtures make it possible to reorganize the shop as needed.

▲ **Figure 3:** Sharp, action angles are complemented by rounded surfaces to create the desired sense of movement—and excitement—generated by the game of soccer.

▲ **Figure 4:** The flocking station is where fans can get their garments personalized and is another way customer interaction is encouraged in the store.

▲ **Figure 5:** Always leave them winning! Shoppers at the multi-station checkout are enveloped by a giant mural of a winning play and cheering all the way back to the stadium.

CASE STUDY 4.10

CASA PALACIO

SANTA FÉ, MEXICO CITY, MEXICO

DESIGN: JEFFREY HUTCHISON & ASSOCIATES, NEW YORK CITY, USA

DESIGN OBJECTIVE

Casa Palacio is part of the Palacio de Hierro chain of upscale, elegant department stores in Mexico. Casa Palacio is a modern home emporium, focused on creating an aspirational dream for its customers, providing everything one needs to design, decorate, and furnish a home. This is truly unique as most home stores might offer furniture and decorative accessories but not appliances or design studio services. Jeffrey Hutchison of Jeffrey Hutchison & Associates, an architectural design firm based in New York City, was called upon to design the newest outlet for this chain in a 60,000 sq. ft, three-level addition to the Centro Santa Fé Mall. This store is targeted at the increasing number of affluent shoppers in Mexico. Hutchison explains: "In most cases, the client has a general brand story, but there are numerous ways to interpret that story in a built environment. I look for creative ways to marry unique design elements with the client's brand story, thereby establishing a niche in the marketplace which allows our client's brand to stand out. When we are asked by a client to update their brand, we try and maintain some of the key original design elements but give them a new look. Therefore, there are still aspects of a store's design that are familiar to the customer."

DESIGN SOLUTION

Jeffrey Hutchison explains how he approached this project: "It is important for us to establish the story behind the brand. We start with the product and what the client is trying to communicate to their customer with those designs. Then we research design inspirations—photos of architecture, interiors, sculpture, art, nature, etc.—along with material research. He continues: "In order to capture the breadth of the store's offerings, we created two different and distinct worlds. The first is a modern market, or bazaar, which is inspired by the great markets of Europe. The market is the main entry and arrival point for all customers and it houses all items needed to 'outfit' one's home, inclusive of kitchen utensils, appliances, food products, etc. The second world we created was a 'street' of houses. After leaving the market, the customer moves towards the natural lit street with five houses of distinct and different style, two of which are modern and three classic, including a mansion townhouse at the end of the street. The customer enters one of the houses and finds him- or herself in a completely different world. Each house is completely furnished in styles that match the house's façade. The customers are in fact transported. This allows for an aspirational connection to the product and enhances the opportunities for multiple sales."

It is important for the style of the store to set the right tone for the brand:

> *We "merged" classic vocabulary with modern elements. For example, the market is designed with many classic details such as terracotta tile walls and floor, but then we inserted a modern wood sculptural canopy into the space, which ties the entire space together. The materials used also reinforce this juxtaposition. We used classic materials to reinforce those styles, but then we also used natural materials to give a more comforting and residential feel. We did not want anything that was manmade or manufactured. It was also important to include fire and water in the project—again, to reinforce the idea of home. So, we designed a central fireplace in the market and we included a water wall feature in the street. I believe that interacting with all of the senses is critical to create the strongest connection between the brand's story and the customer. Smell and sound, as well as visual stimulation, is key. I would also say that the use of natural elements such as water and fire are also important to creating an emotional connection with the customer. Of course, all of these elements need to relate to the message of the brand and the story being told. All of these elements are combined to create an exciting shopping experience for the home.*

When Jeffrey Hutchison is asked how he, as the designer, turns a two-dimensional brand statement into a three-dimensional environment, he responds: "It starts with finding the appropriate inspiration images and materials that support the story narrative we are trying to create. Many designers work in this same manner, including fashion designers. Then we set out to reinterpret the inspiration in a way that is new and relevant to the brand itself. We never 'copy' another design. We study each design element of the space inclusive of the architecture, lighting, fixtures, displays, etc. to shape and fashion it into something unique in the marketplace."

CONCLUSION

When asked, "Since this store is in the very upscale Santa Fé neighborhood of Mexico City, is a prototype design something we will be seeing in the near future?" Hutchison replies: "It is not intended to be 'rolled out,' per se. There will be other future locations, but given the size of the project, the exact store will not be able to be recreated in all of those sites. Instead, critical design elements that establish the brand's message will be repeated and introduced in these future stores. For example, each location will have a market and a street of houses. The configuration may be different. The materials used and special design features like the sculptural wood canopy in the market will also be adapted for these new stores."

DESIGN CREDITS:

Design:	Jeffrey Hutchison & Associates, New York City, USA Jeffrey Hutchison: President and Owner
Client:	Casa Palacio / Palacio de Hierro
Photography:	Jeffrey Hutchison & Associates

▲ **Figure 1:** Set in the three-story addition to the upscale mall in the Santa Fé district of Mexico City is the new Casa Palacio. The design consists of two distinct worlds. Shown here is the "To Market" area: a contemporary twist on Mexican and European markets.

▲ **Figure 2:** A modern lattice structure becomes a canopy for the small individual shops. The wood sculptural element also ties the area together. To reinforce the home theme, there is a fireplace in the center of the market.

▶ **Figure 3:** A "street" of houses makes up the second world, lit from above with natural light streaming in through the skylight. Five houses of different styles—three classic and two modern—fill the "street."

◀ **Figure 4:** At the end of the "street" stands a mansion townhouse. Each house is completely furnished in styles matching the façade. To complement the fireplace in the market, there is a fountain on the street, thus completely the "fire and water" concept of home.

◀ **Figure 5:** Throughout, the design reinforces the juxtaposing of classic and contemporary elements and materials. "Manmade or manufactured" was replaced by "natural" to give a more comforting and residential feel to the space.

◀ **Figure 6:** Each house is furnished in the style suited to that suggested by the exterior design of the façade. "This allows for an aspirational connection to the products and enhances opportunities for multiple sales."

CASE STUDY 4.11

SWAROVSKI

BASEL, SWITZERLAND

DESIGN: TOKUJIN YOSHIOKA, JAPAN

DESIGN OBJECTIVE

Over the past 100 years Swarovski has built a brand that now has its products sold in over 170 countries. Swarovski designs, manufactures, and globally markets high quality crystal and crystal-related products. Since its establishment in 1895, the firm has adhered to the philosophy of extending its offer to a wider customer base. Robert Buchbauer, a member of Swarovski's Executive Board, says: "Today, Swarovski is the most visible global fashion jewelry brand, and our goal is to increase global awareness with a consistent premium status in all markets. The Swarovski Consumer Goods Business stands for premium fashion jewelry and the world's finest crystal—a unique combination of beauty, quality and accessibility: heritage and craftsmanship can also be innovative and on-trend. Reinforcing this image is one of Swarovski's key assets."

For the brand's appearance at Baselworld, a giant trade fair in Basel, Switzerland, the firm asked the noted Japanese architect/designer Tokujin Yoshioka to create the breathtaking stand in which Swarovski's watch and fashion jewelry collections were displayed. It was to be "brand new and innovative" and to be the most exciting stand at the fair. The immense circular exhibit covered more than 2000 sq. meters (approx. 21,500 sq. ft) on two levels.

DESIGN SOLUTION

Here is how Tokujin Yoshioka saw the brand, how he interpreted it and realized it in all its shimmering splendor:

> *I was asked to create a brand-new and innovative design representing the characteristic of Swarovski. When I first started to work with them (over eight years ago) I learned the history of Swarovski crystals and spent more time on a dialogue with the materials. I was drawn to the sparkle and beauty of crystals which harmoniously form the brand philosophy. I am fascinated with its poetic transparency, and the beauty of the material which could capture light and sparkle even as it is transparent itself, and its ability to be a chameleon—always reinventing itself with the seasons, the trends, the moods.*

The original idea behind the stand was to create the space from the luminance itself. Imagine a swan on a lake spreading its wings gracefully as a symbol of Swarovski (the swan is Swarovski's brand signature concept). The façade expresses Swarovski's "world of luminance" by drawing the great curvature and creating the dynamic space of light. The sparkle wall emits the strong and elegant glow like a swan spreading its wings gracefully. My intention was to express the space by the dazzle of light, and not by forms. Visitors would enter the world of Swarovski by being veiled with light of luminance.

The great curved outer shell is made up of 253,231 60 mm hexagonal metal reflectors which "symbolize the facets of the Swarovski crystals," while 22,856 LEDs are skillfully positioned to create the dazzling lighting effects via a computer program. The desired effect, according to the designer, "is how sunlight dances on the water." Yoshioka continues: "To reflect the sweep and dynamic quality of the outer surface, there is a crystal wall (on the interior) that also serves as a dividing element between the open stand and the VIP and bar areas." A total of 34,000 cut crystals, produced by Swarovski in Wattens, Austria, were used to surface the wall in the same hexagonal pattern that was introduced on the exterior wall. Yoshioka designed the 40 freestanding showcases in which the brand products were displayed: "My inspiration for the design of the showcases came from the shape of the crystal structure and was produced in the hexagonal shape in assorted heights."

CONCLUSION

In summing up his thoughts on the Swarovski stand at Baselworld Yoshioka says: "When I design, I do not design internally. It is important to design something expressed in time and for the senses. I think about how I tell the message (the brand philosophy). With Swarovski, I think it is the sparkle that is more loved than the crystal and I created a design that expressed that point. This 'Wings of Sparkle' stand will remain a prototype."

Speaking for the Swarovski Group, Nathalie Colin, Creative Director, Consumer Goods Division, says: "Baselworld remains very key as a window to our overall brand. We wanted the visitors to be surprised by our brand-new stand which is quite innovative this year. Our design criterion takes a new dimension and made once more the most of our expertise to mingle harmoniously with the well-known excellence of Swiss watch-making."

DESIGN CREDITS:

Design:	Tokujin Yoshioka, Japan
Client:	Swarovski Group
	Robert Buchbauer: Member of Swarovski's Executive Board
	Nathalie Colin: Creative Director, Consumer Goods Division
Photography:	Courtesy of the Swarovski Group

▶ **Figure 1:** This gigantic two-story exhibit made a shimmering presence at Baselworld in which Swarovski watches and jewelry were featured.

▶ **Figure 2:** This wall "reflects the sweep and dynamic quality of the outer surface" and also serves as a dividing element between the open stand and the VIP and bar areas. The image shows some of the 34,000 cut crystals used to surface the walls of the exhibit.

◀ **Figure 3:** The back of the circular outer drum with recessed niches for the product displays at eye level. Again, the Swarovski name and logo relieve the sparkling surface.

◀ **Figure 4:** The freestanding showcases shown here were inspired by the hexagonal crystal structures used to surface the walls of the exhibit structure.

▲ **Figure 5:** A close-up of some of the 253,231 hexagonal metal reflectors that make up the outer wall and "symbolize the facets of Swarovski crystals."

Conclusion

WHAT THE ARCHITECTS AND DESIGNERS HAD TO SAY

With more and more online brands doing so well, why would any brand go to the trouble and expense of creating a brick-and-mortar brand identity? The answer is really quite obvious—or it should be, after looking at the pictures and reading about what the brands in this book went through, why they did what they did, and what the results have accomplished for the brand. Yes, one could create a new website to highlight new elements or products or strategies for the brand, but would that get the message across as well as the actual experience of entering a new space which is designed to appeal to all the potential customer's senses? The brand identities that were created for the brands we have collected in this volume are strong and vital and satisfy each brand's desire to show off a new look for the company, or open it up to a new shopper, or make it relevant in a new area or country. Most important is the fact that the shopper or diner or potential client can actually see, touch, feel, smell, and be physically and emotionally involved with the brand and its products in a real-time experience.

From the various architects and designers who delivered the projects in this book, one can see how the design process works. First and foremost: Who and/or what is the brand? And then: What does it hope to accomplish with this new three-dimensional identity? As the designers of the revitalized Monton brand put it, "It is essential to analyze the attributes and characteristics of the brand carefully and understand it in depth before it is possible to create a new brand identity." Once the designer understands the brand and the brand's objective—what it hopes the new design will accomplish—"studying" is next on the design team's agenda. As the designers of Medi said, "We do quite a bit of studying. We look at other brands in the same sector, we look at the space for historical references; we look at the immediate neighborhood to see what is there and what might be lacking. We look for inspiration completely outside of the brand. Sometimes the freshest looks are those derived from something completely unexpected."

When the brand moves into a new country, the designers must learn about what can and what cannot be done in that culture, what to bring along from the parent country and what has to be adapted to the new market. Wrangler brings elements of the American Wild West to Germany knowing that the hip shoppers will "get it" and find symbols like the pony skin stools, painted *faux* Navajo blanket/rug, and stars-and-stripes fabric drapery fun. It wouldn't be Galeries Lafayette for the upscale shoppers in Jakarta without decorative elements of Beaux-Arts architecture and iconic elements like a skeletal Eiffel Tower and fixtures based on Parisian kiosks. However, the designers of PUMA in Osaka acknowledge the Japanese location and community with the use of traditional materials and minimal design. Origami-like details are added to make the customers feel more at home.

Where the brand reaches out to new markets—oftentimes younger shoppers or more upscale trade—the designers need to retain enough of the original signature elements to keep and maintain its faithful customers. The designers of the Karl Lagerfeld London flagship store explain: "The store design is required to find a way of communicating the changes and convincing the existing customer base of the benefits related to these changes. The communication should include certain aspects that conform to a certain level of familiarity and trust with the brand so it is easier for the existing customer base to follow the changes."

For those who have the product but have not yet established the brand—the projects we have included in our "A Brand Is Born" section—the designer is often quite free in creating the brand as well as the identity. The design team of Medi was challenged to provide it all. "It was wide open and it was up to us to develop the language, the colors—the brand. We often seek out projects which are very loose and very open in terms of brand and look. We like to get involved on the ground level and work up from there." Explaining the approach taken to create the brand and brand identity for apple & pie, the children's shoe store, the designer said: "The clients were not sure about how to brand the new business. This is the moment we stepped in—to create a concept. We believe it is important that we find out what the clients want and in this case it was a shop that is fun for kids and at the same time provides shoes that fit for the healthy growth of young feet. The giant apples and the pies are not only eye-catching but they are the symbol of health for growing young people."

When I started this book, I sent out a questionnaire to the many architects and designers I have had the pleasure and honor of working with as the editor of a design magazine and the author/editor of numerous books on retail design and visual merchandising. Basically, the purpose of the questionnaire was to have architects/designers—in their own words—describe the process by which they serve their clients in creating successful brand identities. As projects were being submitted, I also became acquainted with many new, young designers and design firms. I hope you found these different brands interesting and diverse in their quests for brand identities, and in how they achieved their desired objectives thanks to the contributions of the talented architects and designers who contributed these projects. Also, I offer my profound THANK YOU to all the photographers who shared their views of these projects to make these a feast for the eye as well, as I hope, food for thought and possible inspiration.

As an example of the material I was fortunate to receive, I would like to conclude with the answers provided by Werner Franz (CEO and founder of plajer & franz studio of Berlin) and his staff to my questionnaire. He and his team are the architectural designers of the Karl Lagerfeld, Galeries Lafayette, and PUMA Osaka stores in this book. I think these rather full and direct answers are in many ways typical of how many architects and designers create store designs that are fine examples of a brand's identity.

When starting a project, does the client provide you with its brand statement: Who it is? What it stands for? Where it came from (heritage/tradition)? Where it is going (looking to appeal to a new audience)? Visual cues (signature colors, logo, graphics, display, or VM technique, etc.)?

As a matter of fact, this information is crucial. Today a store concept is about reflecting the DNA of the brand, including its character, heritage, its spirit, its vision and mission. This requires, of course, numerous meetings in order to discuss these issues in depth before starting with the design process. The same applies to any aspects of the brand's graphic elements that quite often are being developed by an external creative agency.

Accordingly, this information has to be given, and if it is not included in the brief, we have to discuss it in preliminary meetings. In addition, we have to do our own research to learn about the external effect of the brand and the way it is perceived. Occasionally, this might differ from the image the brand has of itself. Moreover, it is important to do our own research in order to find out where the brand is positioned and who is the competition, and also get to know the brand's communication so far (this includes also the outer appearance in the form of store and headquarters design) and if it has been done in accordance with the DNA.

It is important that the brand knows itself. Occasionally this is not the case and happens progressively during the cooperation process.

Store design is a form of communication; it simply does not work without knowing the brand inside and out.

This applies to the cooperation with all our clients, be it PUMA, KARL LAGERFELD, Galeries Lafayette, BMW, or other brands.

When you are working with a new client that has no real or recognized brand and you are expected to help create one—how do you approach that situation?

In such case you basically start at an earlier stage. Together with the client we work out the DNA of his label. Here, plajer & franz studio is involved in the developing process and cooperatively works out the philosophy, the message, and corporate design of the brand.

This is a particularly interesting process that requires a vibrant exchange of ideas. It also requires a lot of research into the environment that the brand would be placed in and asks us to be very critical of both the client's ideas and the reality out there.

Creating a DNA of a brand is, however, a very inspiring creative process and in such cases the development of the store design might proceed parallel to the searching for a brand identity. Sometimes certain ideas for the store design—single visuals, material ideas, spatial arrangements—might influence the brand character.

How do you take this information and reinterpret it in 3-D: in the colors you select, the textures, the materials, forms, choice of fixtures, fittings, and furniture?

At plajer & franz studio, this process usually begins with sketches (hand drawings) in which first ideas are put down on paper and the first vision of the space is created. Various options are being tested, alienated, and played with. At the point where the imagination of sketches—2-D—reaches its limits, you move on to transform the ideas into three-dimensional visualizations. 3-D allows for a better comprehension of the space and the ideas for the design of it and offers the kind of "look & feel." Colors, textures, materials, and other design elements are not always chosen at the same stage; it varies. Though some of these design elements are already visible in the hand drawings, sometimes the ideas for materials, colors, textures, and fittings evolve in the 3-D process. It is important that all design elements match the character and DNA of the brand!

This is particularly visible in the stores we have designed for PUMA, in which the spirit of the brand is visible and perceptible throughout. The stores are literally "PUMA-rized." The same applies to KARL LAGERFELD: the black and white images, a minimalistic and simple design reflect the DNA of the brand.

What sensory cues can be added to explain or enhance the brand: aroma, music, displays, food tasting, etc?

This strongly depends on the character of the brand. Of course, a store design wants to approach the consumers on an emotional level, hence it usually includes certain sensory aspects—these can be materials, colors, surfaces but also aromas and, of course, music! They are all part of the brand's identity and its communication with consumers.

Generally, sensory cues have to match the character of the brand and type of merchandise it offers. Sometimes it should also respect the local relevance of where the store is placed and what is its origin. Serving colorful macaroons in a "Marie Antoinette" French-style fashion boutique could be a great asset. It would add to the shopping experience. However, in a store that sells Japanese, minimalistic fashion even the slightest idea of bringing a "playful" element into the store would seem extraneous—unless this Japanese brand opens a store in Paris and chooses macaroons in black and white, matching the collection sold in-store or ventures out into bright pink ones as a super contrast ... This might add to a "cool" appearance.

How important to establishing the fashion brand are the mannequins or forms that are used? The lighting?

Any form of visual display element has an important role in creating a coherent appearance of the store. It is not only the interior architecture that creates the (brand) store image, but the visual merchandising and the above-mentioned sensory cues as well. All these aspects have to correspond and complement each other. Lighting is a crucial aspect of store architecture, whereas mannequins are a vital part of visual merchandising. It is important that neither store architecture nor visual merchandising nor any other elements in-store overshadows the product!!! Their main role is to highlight the product and create an adequate stage for it. The product is the star that presents itself on this stage. Lighting is another—and a particularly important—means to create the theatrical atmosphere. Hence, in store design architecture, differentiated light levels are used all over the space. It is placed and adjusted so as to accentuate certain elements and highlight important areas and, of course, it is used to highlight the star on stage!

If updating or upscaling an established brand—expanding the target market—how do you retain the existing customer base? What do you maintain and what do you change?

In fact this is the role of the brand and its marketing specialists ... as it requires aspects that include the product design, packaging, and of course marketing strategies. However, the store design has to support this evolution or transformation as well. Basically, what is required is to find a way of communicating the changes and convincing the existing customer base of the benefits related to these changes. The communication should include certain aspects that confirm a certain level of familiarity and trust with the brand so that it is easier for the existing customer base to follow the changes. As already mentioned, this needs to be included in the general brand communication (products, brand message in ads, marketing, PR, etc.) but should also be a part of the store design—for example, a single element that is familiar, a similar consumer journey, a social aspect and so on …

If this is a prototype that will eventually be rolled out across the country or around the world—how do you accommodate the design to new spaces and cultures and ethnicities?

Usually—or at least this is the experience we have made so far at plajer & franz studio—it is known from the beginning if a store design concept is intended for a regional or international rollout. In such a case we develop a prototype that is usually a "premium concept" and reflects the best option possible for the brand. Here the choice of materials and aesthetic elements is usually at the highest possible level. The "premium concept" is mainly intended for a flagship or premium brand store. On the global playground, this prototype should leave room for certain creative elements or materials that respond to cultural and ethnic differences—for example, the aspect of local relevance in our PUMA stores in Osaka, Amsterdam, London, Munich, Paris, etc.

However, a rollout also requires adjustments on different levels. Usually we have a few premium stores located in the world's metropolitan cities and a large number of "normal" brand stores. The design for a brand store follows different specifications, mainly in relation to budget, surface size, material choice, and some country-specific requirements. Therefore, the premium prototype undergoes a so-called "downgrading" process to meet these requirements. Within the downgrading process other local, cultural and ethnic aspects are being respected. These include varying production costs depending on the economic and social aspects of the country as well as country-specific material selection (locally produced materials; material costs, import costs; material endurance respective of climate; ecological aspects; heritage aspects, etc.). Moreover, cultural aspects need to be given respective attention, as for example meanings of certain symbols, attitudes, rituals, mentalities, etc.

The brand is an established fashion house or department store that, in turn, is home to a variety of known brands or designer labels. How does the architect/designer maintain the store's brand identity while still featuring the individual sub-brands? In the case of a brand that has its own selection of sub-brands—how does the designer approach that situation?

Department stores demand special design concepts, as for example our "Galeries Lafayette" project in Jakarta and Berlin. Here we have a stand-alone brand—the department store—and multiple sub-brands with diverse, individual images, characters, and visual appearances. Quite often the mistake is being made that either one brand of the department store or the individual sub-brands dominate and either one is not being given the respective attention. What it needs is to find a way in which all remain autonomous while being integrated into a single unit. The design concept plajer & franz studio developed for Galeries Lafayette aimed at giving the brand "Galeries Lafayette" full attention, presenting it in full scope while reflecting its DNA, character, and heritage. When you enter the department store in Jakarta or in Berlin (here we have redesigned the ground floor in 2012) you will immediately receive the feeling of being in Galeries Lafayette, the fashion temple with strong French heritage. And yet, the sub-brands have their own presence! The department store brand should create a frame for the sub-brands. You can compare it with a painting and the impact it has depending on the frame. A well-chosen frame does not distract from the content of the painting; it emphasizes it while being visible and presents itself as well.

Moreover, as a department store is diverse and huge in size, it needs not only to take over the "framing" role but also give re-emerging focus points to create a consumer journey and help the customer find their way.

Also—and very important—is to keep customers interested during their visit. Surprising elements should frequently appear and should be placed on each of the floors. A bored and confused customer will leave the department store without proceeding to further floors. And in fact, it is one of the main challenges in retail to actually persuade the consumer to proceed to the upper floors. This challenge is already great in respect to two-floor shops, as was the case in respect to the PUMA store in Osaka. For huge department stores like Galeries Lafayette, this challenge is even greater and refers to both directions—up and down—as many shoppers start with the upper floor.

Based on the final look and feel of the brand environment that was created, how does the architect/designer judge the result? What was the client's reaction? How about the public's response?

Basically, the public's response is the evaluation of the store design. At the same time it pronounces its judgment about the cooperation between client and architect, which, as a matter of fact, is a vital factor for success or failure respectively. The client's reaction is based on the reaction of the consumers and how they respond in terms of verbal compliments, frequency, and shopping behavior. The architect judges the result by testing whether his/her visual ideas work in practice the way he/she imagined they would.

Appendix: List of Designers

Thank you to all the designers and design firms who contributed to this book.

adidas, Space Ninety 8, Williamsburg, Brooklyn, New York, USA

Roundhouse, 537 SE Ash St #401, Portland, Oregon, USA

Aéropostale, Roosevelt Field, Long Island, New York, USA

GH+A Design, 1100 avenue des Canadiens-de-Montreal, Suite 130, Montreal, Quebec H3B 2S2, Canada

Allen Solly, Bangalore, India

Dalziel + Pow, 5–8 Hardwick Street, London EC1R 4RG, UK

apple & pie, One South Island, Hong Kong, China

Stefano Tordiglione Design Ltd., 3/F, 37 Staunton Street, Soho, Central Hong Kong, China

Baccarat, Madison Avenue, New York City, USA

Rafael de Cardenas / Architecture at Large, 611 Broadway, Suite 627, New York City 10012, USA

Barbican, Barbican Centre, London, UK

SHH Architects, 1 Vencourt Place, Ravenscourt Park, London W6 9NU, UK

Barbisio Factory, Catania, Italy

DUO Commercial Design, Piazza V. Emanuele lll, n.24, Piano ll, 95129, Catania, Italy

Bell, Toronto, Canada

Burdifilek, 183 Bathurst Street, Suite #300, Toronto M5T 2R7, Canada

Ben Sherman, Carnaby Street, London, UK

Brinkworth, 4–5 Ellsworth Street, London E2 0AX, UK

Buffalo Wild Wings, Cincinnati, Ohio, USA

FITCH, 585 S. Front Street, Columbus, Ohio 43215, USA

Camper, Fifth Avenue, New York City, USA

Nendo, 2-2-16-6F, Shimomeguro Meguro-ku, Tokyo 153-0064, Japan

Camper, Shanghai, China

Neri & Hu, 88 Yuqing Road, Shanghai 200030, China

Carlo Pazolini, Broadway, SoHo, New York City, USA

Giorgio Borruso Design, 333 Washington Boulevard #352, Marina del Rey, California 90292, USA

Casa Palacio, Santa Fé, Mexico City, Mexico

Jeffrey Hutchison & Associates, 435 Hudson Street, New York City 10014, USA

Central Kitchen, San Francisco, California, USA

Paxton Gate, 824 Valencia Street, San Francisco, California 94110, USA

Cortefiel, Seville, Spain

JGA, 29110 Inkster Road, Southfield, Michigan 48034, USA

Domino's, Houston, Texas, USA

Chute Gerdeman, 455 S. Ludlow Street, Columbus, Ohio 43215, USA

DORMA, The BAU Fair, Munich, Germany

dan pearlman Markenarchitektur, Kiefholzstrasse 1, 12435 Berlin, Germany

Double Wide Grill, Adams Township, Pennsylvania, USA

Gruskin Group, 294 Morris Avenue, Springfield, New Jersey 07081, USA

être belle, Frankfurt, Germany

Blocher Blocher Shops, Herdweg 19, 70174 Stuttgart, Germany

FC Bayern Fan Shop, Allianz Arena, Munich, Germany

Gruschwitz GmbH, Tizianstrasse 53, D-80638, Munich, Germany

Galeries Lafayette, Pacific Place Mall, Jakarta, Indonesia

plajer & franz studio, Erkelenzdamm 59, 10999 Berlin, Germany

Great Dane, Redfern, Sydney, Australia

McCartney Design, The Bayer Building, 275 Alfred St. North, Suite #502, North Sydney, New South Wales 2060, Australia

House of Kipling, 29 Brompton Road, London, UK

UXUS, Keizersgracht 174-V, 1016 DW Amsterdam, The Netherlands

hr2, Brossard Quartier Dix 30, Quebec City, Canada

Janson Goldstein LLP, 180 Varick Street, New York City 10014, USA

JanSport, Mall of Georgia, Buford, Georgia, USA
Twenty Four 7, 425 NE 9th Avenue, Portland, Oregon 97232, USA

Joe Fresh, Fifth Avenue, New York City, USA
Burdifilek, 183 Bathurst Street, Suite #300, Toronto M5T 2R7, Canada

KARL LAGERFELD London, Regent Street, London, UK
plajer & franz studio, Erkelenzdamm 59, 10999 Berlin, Germany

Maidenform, Santiago, Chile
Droguett A&A Ltd., Padre Mariano 10, of.306, Providencia, Santiago, Chile

McCormick World of Flavors, Harborplace, Light Street Pavilion, Baltimore, Maryland, USA
JGA, 29110 Inkster Road, Southfield, Michigan 48034, USA

Medi, Arlington, Virginia, USA
GrizForm Design Architects, 1611 Connecticut Avenue NW, Washington, DC 20009, USA

Monton, St. Petersburg, Russia
dan pearlman Markenarchitektur, Kiefholzstrasse 1, 12435 Berlin, Germany

Oakville Grocery, St. Helena Highway, Oakville, Napa Valley, California, USA
Avila Design, 2471 Shattuck Avenue, Berkeley, California 94704, USA

PUMA, Osaka, Japan
plajer & franz studio, Erkelenzdamm 59-61, 10999 Berlin, Germany

PUMA Factory Outlet Center, Carlsbad, California, USA
Colkitt&Co Architects, 2479 Kettner Boulevard, San Diego, California 92101, USA

Qela, The Pearl, Dohar, Qatar
UXUS, Keizersgracht 174-V, 1016 DW Amsterdam, The Netherlands

Rodd & Gunn, Noosa, Australia
Pennant & Triumph, PO Box 27-807, Mount Roskill, Auckland 1440, New Zealand

Sal Curioso, Wyndham Street, Hong Kong, China
Stefano Tordiglione Design Ltd., 3/F, 37 Staunton Street, Soho, Central Hong Kong, China

Sandbar, Anna Maria Island, Florida, USA
The Schimberg Group, 40 South Pineapple Avenue #101, Sarasota, Florida 34236, USA

Solara, Carrefour Richelieu, Saint-Jean-sur-Richelieu, Quebec, Canada

Ruscio Studio, 2197 Rue Sherbrooke E., Montreal, Quebec H2K 1C8, Canada

Susanna Pizzeria, Bleecker Street, Greenwich Village, New York City, USA

Sergio Mannino Studio, 45 Main Street #546, Brooklyn, New York City 11201, USA

Swarovski, Basel, Switzerland

Tokujin Yoshioka, 150-0034 Daikanyama-cho 9-1, Shibuya-ku, Tokyo, Japan

Vince Camuto, Grand Central Station, East 42nd Street, New York City, USA

Sergio Mannino Studio, 45 Main Street #546, Brooklyn, New York City 11201, USA

Wawa, Central Florida

CBX, 36 East 21st Street, New York City 10010, USA

Whole Foods, Mack Avenue, Detroit, Michigan, USA

JGA, 29110 Inkster Road, Southfield, Michigan 48034, USA

Wrangler, Leipzig, Germany

Checkland Kindleysides, Charnwood Edge, Cossington, Leicester, LE7 4U2, UK

Youtopia, Ravensburg, Germany

dan pearlman Markenarchitektur, Kiefholzstrasse 1, 12435, Berlin, Germany